Electric Skillet

Cookbook

200 Recipes that will make your mouth water for the best BPA-free nonstick cookware that saves energy

By

Geneva Lewellen

TABLE OF CONTENT

INTRODUCTION

Introducing you to the world of easy and flexible cooking with the "Electric Skillet Cookbook." This culinary adventure is intended for home cooks who value the versatility and efficiency that an electric skillet offers them in the kitchen.

This cookbook delves into the countless ways you may cook delectable dishes with an electric skillet—a contemporary kitchen marvel that combines the capabilities of an oven and a stovetop into one small gadget. This cookbook is your go-to resource for learning the art of cooking with an electric skillet, regardless of your level of experience in the kitchen or desire to try new recipes.

You'll find a wide range of dishes that suit different palates and dietary requirements there. Every recipe, which ranges from filling breakfasts to flavorful meals and sweet treats, is designed to highlight the amazing variety of foods that can be made with ease in your electric skillet. The dishes are great for families and busy people looking for tasty homemade dinners without all the hassle because they're quick and easy to prepare.

The "Electric Skillet Cookbook" is your go-to resource in the kitchen, whether you're cooking for one person or entertaining a large group of people. Come along with us as we set out on a culinary journey to discover how to get the most out of your electric skillet and turn common items into amazing dinners.

Prepare to transform your culinary adventures and relish the delight of crafting delectable recipes with the "Electric Skillet Cookbook." Start the pungent, sizzling trip now!

BREAKFAST DELIGHTS:

SUNRISE SCRAMBLE STACK:

Ingredients:

- 4 large eggs
- 1/4 cup milk
- Salt and pepper to taste
- 1 tablespoon butter
- 1 cup diced tomatoes
- 1 cup diced bell peppers
- 1 cup shredded cheddar cheese
- Chopped chives for garnish

Instructions:

1. Add eggs, milk, salt, and pepper to a bowl and mix them using a whisk.
2. In a pan over medium heat, melt the butter. Mix the eggs and add them.
3. Add the diced tomatoes and bell peppers when the eggs start to set.
4. Scramble the eggs slowly until they are done.
5. Put cheddar cheese shreds on top and let them melt.
6. Put the scramble on a plate and top it with chopped chives.

BLUEBERRY BLISS PANCAKES:

Ingredients:

- 1 cup all-purpose flour
- 2 tablespoons sugar
- 1 teaspoon baking powder
- 1/2 teaspoon baking soda

- 1/4 teaspoon salt
- 3/4 cup buttermilk
- 1 large egg
- 2 tablespoons melted butter
- 1 cup fresh blueberries

Instructions:

1. Mix the flour, sugar, baking powder, baking soda, and salt in a bowl with a whisk.
2. Mix the egg, melted butter, and buttermilk in a different bowl using a whisk.
3. Add the wet ingredients to the dry ones and mix them just until they are mixed.
4. Add the blueberries slowly and carefully.
5. Set a pan or grill over medium heat. For every pancake, pour 1/4 cup of batter.
6. Once the top starts to bubble, flip it over and cook until golden brown.
7. You can serve it with maple sugar and extra blueberries if you want.

AVOCADO TOAST EXTRAVAGANZA:

Ingredients:

- 2 slices whole-grain bread
- 1 ripe avocado
- Salt and pepper to taste
- Red pepper flakes (optional)
- Poached eggs (optional)
- Cherry tomatoes, sliced (optional)

Instructions:

1. How you like it, toast the bread slices.

2. Set the ripe avocado in a bowl and mash it while the bread toasts.
3. On top of the toasted bread, spread the mashed avocado out equally.
4. Add pepper and salt. If you want some heat, add red pepper flakes.
5. If you want, you can add poached eggs and chopped cherry tomatoes on top.

SPINACH AND FETA OMELETTE:

Ingredients:

- 3 large eggs
- 1 tablespoon olive oil
- 1 cup fresh spinach, chopped
- 1/4 cup crumbled feta cheese
- Salt and pepper to taste

Instructions:

1. Whisk the eggs together in a bowl.
2. In a nonstick pan over medium heat, heat the olive oil.
3. Put chopped spinach in the pan and cook it until it wilts.
4. Add the eggs that have been beaten to the spinach.
5. After the eggs have set a bit, put feta cheese on one side of them.
6. After you fold the omelette in half, cook it until the eggs are set through.
7. Add pepper and salt to taste.
8. Put the omelette on a plate and serve it.

BANANA NUT MUFFIN MAGIC:

Ingredients:

- 2 cups all-purpose flour
- 1 teaspoon baking soda
- 1/2 teaspoon salt
- 1/2 cup unsalted butter, softened
- 1 cup granulated sugar
- 2 large eggs
- 1 teaspoon vanilla extract
- 3 ripe bananas, mashed
- 1/2 cup chopped nuts (walnuts or pecans)

Instructions:

1. Warm your oven to 350°F (175°C) and put paper liners in a muffin pan.
2. Mix the flour, baking soda, and salt in a medium-sized bowl using a whisk.
3. In a different big bowl, beat the butter and sugar until they are fluffy and light. Add the eggs and beat well after each one, one at a time. Add the vanilla extract and mix well.
4. Add the mashed bananas and mix until everything is well mixed.
5. Slowly add the dry ingredients to the wet ones until everything is mixed. Add the chopped nuts and mix them in.
6. Fill up each muffin cup about two-thirds of the way to the top with batter.
7. Please put it in the oven and bake for 18 to 20 minutes or until a toothpick stuck in the middle comes out clean.
8. Let the muffins cool for 5 minutes in the pan before moving them to a wire rack to cool down.

CINNAMON ROLL FRENCH TOAST:

Ingredients:

- 4 large eggs
- 1 cup milk
- 1 teaspoon vanilla extract
- 1/2 teaspoon ground cinnamon
- 8 slices of day-old cinnamon rolls
- Maple syrup and powdered sugar for serving

Instructions:

1. The eggs, milk, vanilla extract, and ground cinnamon should all be mixed in a small dish.
2. Put a griddle or nonstick pan on medium heat with the heat on high.
3. Coat both sides of a slice of a day-old cinnamon roll with the egg mixture.
4. On a hot skillet, cook the slices on each side for two to three minutes or until golden brown.
5. Put powdered sugar on top of each slice of French toast and serve them with maple syrup.

GREEK YOGURT PARFAIT PERFECTION:

Ingredients:

- 1 cup Greek yogurt
- 1 cup granola
- 1 cup mixed berries (strawberries, blueberries, raspberries)

Instructions:

1. Put 1/3 cup of Greek yoghurt in a bowl or glass.
2. Put 1/3 cup of granola on top of the chocolate milk.
3. Spread out some mixed berries on top.

4. Do this again and again until the bowl or glass is full.
5. You can put honey on top to make it even sweeter
6. Could you do it again for more amounts?

BREAKFAST BURRITO BONANZA:

Ingredients:

- 4 large flour tortillas
- 8 eggs, scrambled
- 1 cup cooked and diced breakfast sausage or bacon
- 1 cup shredded cheddar cheese
- 1 cup salsa
- Salt and pepper to taste
- Optional toppings: diced tomatoes, sliced avocado, sour cream

Instructions:

1. Scramble the eggs in a pan over medium-low heat until they are done. Add pepper and salt.
2. You can use a dry skillet or the oven to warm the flour tortillas.
3. Put some scrambled eggs in the middle of each wrapper to put the burritos together.
4. On top of the eggs, put some cooked sausage or bacon.
5. Add cheddar cheese shreds on top of the filling.
6. Add a spoonful of salsa and any toppings you want.
7. To make a burrito, fold the tortilla's sides in and roll it up tightly.
8. Serve your Breakfast Burrito Bonanza right away and enjoy it!

QUINOA POWER BOWL:

Ingredients:

- 1 cup quinoa, rinsed
- 2 cups water or vegetable broth
- 1 cup cherry tomatoes, halved
- 1 cup cucumber, diced
- 1 cup bell peppers, diced
- 1/2 cup red onion, finely chopped
- 1/4 cup feta cheese, crumbled
- 1/4 cup Kalamata olives, sliced
- 2 tablespoons olive oil
- 1 tablespoon balsamic vinegar
- Salt and pepper to taste
- Fresh parsley for garnish

Instructions:

1. Follow the directions on the package to cook the quinoa with water or veggie broth.
2. Cooked quinoa, cucumber, bell peppers, red onion, feta cheese, and Kalamata olives should all be put in a big bowl together.
3. Salt and pepper should be mixed with olive oil in a small bowl. Add the dressing to the rice and toss it all together.
4. Before serving, sprinkle with fresh parsley.

COCONUT CHIA PUDDING PARFAIT:

Ingredients:

- 1/4 cup chia seeds
- 1 cup coconut milk
- 1 tablespoon maple syrup or honey
- 1/2 teaspoon vanilla extract
- Fresh berries for topping
- Granola for layering

Instructions:

1. Chia seeds, coconut milk, honey, or maple syrup should all be mixed in a bowl. Please put it in the fridge for at least 30 minutes or overnight to thicken. Make sure to stir it well before putting it in.
2. Place chia pudding, granola, and fresh berries in bowls or cups that can be used for serving.
3. Put more berries on top of the last layer and repeat the steps.

SMOKED SALMON BAGEL BRILLIANCE:

Ingredients:

- 2 bagels, sliced and toasted
- 4 oz smoked salmon
- 1/4 cup cream cheese
- 1 tablespoon capers
- Red onion, thinly sliced
- Fresh dill for garnish
- Lemon wedges

Instructions:

1. Toast the bread halves and spread cream cheese on them.
2. Put smoked salmon, capers, and red onion pieces on top.
3. Serve with lemon wedges and fresh dill on top.

VEGGIE-LOADED BREAKFAST PIZZA:

Ingredients:

- 1 pre-made pizza crust or pizza dough
- 1/2 cup tomato sauce
- 1 cup shredded mozzarella cheese
- 1 bell pepper, thinly sliced

- 1/2 cup cherry tomatoes, halved
- 1/4 cup red onion, thinly sliced
- 1 cup spinach leaves
- 4 large eggs
- Salt and pepper to taste
- Olive oil for drizzling

Instructions:

1. Follow the directions on the pizza crust or dough to heat the oven.
2. On a baking sheet, roll out the pizza crust.
3. Cover the bread with tomato sauce and top it with mozzarella cheese.
4. On top, put red onion, bell pepper, cherry tomatoes, and spinach.
5. Make holes in the vegetables and put an egg in each one.
6. Add pepper and salt.
7. Following the directions on the pizza crust or dough, bake in a hot oven until the eggs are done the way you like them.
8. Add olive oil and sprinkle on top before serving.

APPLE CINNAMON WAFFLE WONDERLAND:

Ingredients:

- 1 cup all-purpose flour
- 1 tablespoon sugar
- 1 teaspoon baking powder
- 1/2 teaspoon baking soda
- 1/4 teaspoon salt
- 1 cup buttermilk
- 1/4 cup unsalted butter, melted
- 1 large egg

- 1 teaspoon vanilla extract
- 1 cup grated apple
- 1 teaspoon ground cinnamon

Instructions:

1. Mix the flour, sugar, baking powder, baking soda, and salt in a large bowl with a whisk.
2. Melt the butter and add the egg, vanilla extract, and buttermilk. Beat the ingredients together in a different bowl.
3. Add the wet ingredients to the dry ones and mix them just until they are mixed. Grate the apple and add the cinnamon.
4. Warm up your waffle pan and follow the directions on the package for how to cook the batter.
5. You can put your favourite toppings on the waffles while they are still warm, like maple syrup, apple slices, or whipped cream.

MEDITERRANEAN BREAKFAST BOWL:

Ingredients:

- 1 cup cooked quinoa
- 1/2 cup cherry tomatoes, halved
- 1/4 cup cucumber, diced
- 1/4 cup red bell pepper, diced
- 2 tablespoons red onion, finely chopped
- 1/4 cup feta cheese, crumbled
- 1 tablespoon olive oil
- 1 tablespoon lemon juice
- Salt and pepper to taste
- Fresh parsley for garnish

Instructions:

1. The cooked quinoa, cherry tomatoes, cucumber, red bell pepper, red onion, and feta cheese should all be put in a bowl together.
2. Mix the lemon juice and olive oil in a small bowl with a whisk. Add pepper and salt to taste.
3. Pour the dressing over the rice and mix it all by tossing it.
4. Add fresh parsley as a garnish and serve right away.

PESTO VEGGIE FRITTATA:

Ingredients:

- 6 large eggs
- 1/4 cup milk
- Salt and pepper to taste
- 1 tablespoon olive oil
- 1/2 cup cherry tomatoes, halved
- 1/2 cup zucchini, diced
- 1/4 cup red bell pepper, diced
- 2 tablespoons pesto sauce
- 1/4 cup feta cheese, crumbled

Instructions:

1. Warm the oven up to 175°F (350°F).
2. Add the eggs, milk, salt, and pepper to a bowl and mix them using a whisk.
3. A pan that can go in the oven should have olive oil. You can also add red bell pepper, zucchini, and green tomatoes. Cook the veggies until they are almost soft.
4. The egg mix should be poured over the veggies in the pan. Put small amounts of pesto sauce on top and top with feta cheese.

5. Place the pan in an oven that has already been heated and bake the frittata for 15 to 20 minutes, or until it is set and golden brown.
6. Grab it from the oven, let it cool, then cut it up and serve.

MANGO TANGO SMOOTHIE BOWL:

Ingredients:

- 1 cup frozen mango chunks
- 1/2 banana
- 1/2 cup Greek yogurt
- 1/2 cup almond milk (or any milk of your choice)
- 1 tablespoon honey (optional, depending on sweetness preference)
- Toppings: sliced mango, granola, chia seeds, shredded coconut

Instructions:

1. Put the frozen mango chunks, banana, Greek yoghurt, almond milk, and honey in a mixer.
2. Add more almond milk to get your desired consistency if you need to. Blend until smooth and creamy.
3. Get a bowl and pour the drink in it.
4. Grass, chia seeds, chopped mango, and shredded coconut should be on top.
5. Have fun drinking your cool Mango Tango Smoothie Bowl!

HUEVOS RANCHEROS FIESTA:

Ingredients:

- 4 large eggs
- 4 corn tortillas

- 1 cup black beans, cooked and drained
- 1 cup salsa (homemade or store-bought)
- 1 cup shredded cheddar or Mexican blend cheese
- 1 avocado, sliced
- 1/4 cup fresh cilantro, chopped
- Salt and pepper to taste
- Olive oil for cooking

Instructions:

1. Warm the tortillas in a dry pan over medium heat until they are soft and warm.
2. Put olive oil in a different pan and heat it over medium-low heat.
3. Keep the eggs separate as you crack them into the pan and cook them however you like (fried or scrambled).
4. Warm up the black beans in a small pot while the eggs cook.
5. To put the dish together, put a tortilla on each plate, then add black beans and an egg on top of each one.
6. Put some salsa on top of each egg, then top with cheese and avocado or chopped cilantro.
7. Add pepper and salt to taste.

BREAKFAST QUESADILLA DELIGHT:

Ingredients:

- 4 large flour tortillas
- 1 cup cooked and crumbled breakfast sausage or bacon
- 1 cup shredded cheddar or Monterey Jack cheese
- 1 cup diced bell peppers (any colour)
- 1/2 cup diced onions
- 4 large eggs, scrambled
- Salt and pepper to taste

- Cooking spray or butter for cooking

Instructions:

1. Fry the bacon or breakfast sausage in a pan over medium-low heat until it's browned and done. Take it out and set it aside.
2. Put some cooking spray or butter in the same pan and add the diced onions and bell peppers. Cook them until they get soft.
3. To make the eggs, just set them in the pan and beat them.
4. Place the tortillas on a flat surface. Scrambled eggs, cooked sausage or bacon, and sautéed veggies should all be put on one half of each tortilla.
5. After adding the cheese to the egg mix, fold the tortillas in half to make a half-moon form.
6. Warm up some cooking spray or butter in a clean pan over medium-low heat. It should be cooked on each side for two to three minutes or until the tortilla is golden brown and the cheese melts.
7. Take them out of the pan and let them cool for one minute. Then, cut them into pieces.
8. Put your favourite salsa, sour cream, or guacamole on the side and serve.

ONE-PAN WONDERS:

LEMON HERB ROASTED CHICKEN:

Ingredients:

- 1 whole chicken (about 4-5 pounds)
- 1/4 cup olive oil
- 2 tablespoons fresh lemon juice
- 2 teaspoons dried thyme

- 2 teaspoons dried rosemary
- 1 teaspoon dried oregano
- Salt and pepper to taste
- 1 lemon, sliced
- 4 cloves garlic, minced

Instructions:

1. Warm the oven up to 190°C (375°F).
2. Olive oil, lemon juice, thyme, rosemary, oregano, salt, and pepper should all be mixed in a small bowl.
3. Put the whole chicken in a pan to cook. Cover the chicken with the herb mixture when you rub it on.
4. Add lemon slices and chopped garlic to the inside of the chicken.
5. When the oven is hot, roast the chicken for about an hour and a half or until the internal temperature hits 165°F (74°C). Every 30 minutes, baste the chicken with the pan juices.
6. After cooking, let the chicken rest for 10 to 15 minutes before cutting it up.

SHRIMP AND ASPARAGUS STIR-FRY:

Ingredients:

- 1 pound large shrimp, peeled and deveined
- 1 bunch asparagus, trimmed and cut into 2-inch pieces
- 2 tablespoons soy sauce
- 1 tablespoon oyster sauce
- 1 tablespoon hoisin sauce
- 1 tablespoon sesame oil
- 2 tablespoons vegetable oil
- 3 cloves garlic, minced
- 1 teaspoon ginger, grated

- Cooked rice for serving

Instructions:

1. Mix soy, oyster, hoisin, and sesame oil in a small bowl. Put away.
2. Put oil from the vegetable pan or wok on medium-high heat.
3. Stir-fry for about 30 seconds after adding the ginger and garlic that have been chopped.
4. Please put in the shrimp and cook them until they get pink.
5. After adding the asparagus, stir-fry for another two to three minutes or until the asparagus is crisp-tender.
6. Put the shrimp and asparagus in a bowl. Add the sauce and stir to coat.
7. Add two to three more minutes of cooking and wait until the shrimp are fully cooked.
8. Put the stir-fry on top of the rice that has already been cooked.

ONE-PAN PESTO SALMON:

Ingredients:

- 4 salmon fillets
- Salt and pepper to taste
- 1/4 cup pesto sauce
- 1 lemon, sliced
- 1 tablespoon olive oil

Instructions:

1. Warm the oven up to 200°C/400°F.
2. Put the salmon pieces on a baking sheet with parchment paper.

3. Add salt and pepper to the salmon.
4. Put a little pesto sauce on top of each salmon piece.
5. Add lemon slices to the salmon.
6. Put some olive oil on top of the salmon.
7. After the hot oven, bake the salmon for 12 to 15 minutes or until it's fully cooked.

TERIYAKI TOFU WITH VEGETABLES:

Ingredients:

- 1 block of firm tofu, pressed and cubed
- 1 cup broccoli florets
- 1 bell pepper, sliced
- 1 carrot, julienned
- 1/4 cup soy sauce
- 2 tablespoons teriyaki sauce
- 1 tablespoon rice vinegar
- 1 tablespoon sesame oil
- 2 tablespoons vegetable oil
- 2 cloves garlic, minced
- 1 teaspoon ginger, grated
- Green onions for garnish
- Cooked rice for serving

Instructions:

1. Mix soy sauce, teriyaki sauce, rice vinegar, and olive oil in a bowl. Put away.
2. Heat vegetable oil in a big pan or wok over medium-high heat.
3. Stir-fry for about 30 seconds after adding the ginger and garlic that have been chopped.
4. Please put in the cubed tofu and cook it all the way through until it turns golden brown.

5. Cut up some broccoli, bell pepper, and carrot into thin strips. To make the greens tender-crisp, stir-fry them for three to four minutes.
6. Pour the sauce over the veggies and tofu, then toss to coat everything. Add two to three more minutes of cooking.
7. Put the veggies and teriyaki tofu on top of cooked rice and top with green onions.

SAUSAGE AND VEGGIE SHEET PAN:

Ingredients:

- 1 pound smoked sausage, sliced
- 1 pound baby potatoes, halved
- 1 bell pepper, sliced
- 1 red onion, sliced
- 1 zucchini, sliced
- 2 tablespoons olive oil
- 1 teaspoon dried oregano
- 1 teaspoon garlic powder
- Salt and pepper to taste

Instructions:

1. Warm the oven up to 200°C/400°F.
2. Put the sliced sausage, baby potatoes cut in half, bell pepper, red onion, and zucchini in a big bowl.
3. Add the olive oil and toss the ingredients to coat them.
4. Add salt, pepper, garlic powder, dried oregano, and more. Again, toss to make sure the spices are spread out evenly.
5. Put the mix on a baking sheet and spread it out evenly.
6. For 25 to 30 minutes, or until the veggies are soft and golden brown, roast them in an oven that has already been heated.

CAJUN CHICKEN AND RICE SKILLET:

Ingredients:

- 1 pound chicken breast, diced
- 1 cup rice
- 1 onion, diced
- 1 bell pepper, diced
- 2 celery stalks, chopped
- 3 cloves garlic, minced
- 2 tablespoons Cajun seasoning
- 1 can (14 oz) diced tomatoes
- 2 cups chicken broth
- Salt and pepper to taste
- Green onions for garnish

Instructions:

1. Boil the chicken until it turns brown in a big pan.
2. Chop up the onion, bell pepper, celery, and garlic and add them. Cook the veggies until they get soft.
3. The rice, diced tomatoes, Cajun spice, and chicken broth should all be stirred.
4. Once the mixture starts to boil, lower the heat, cover, and let it cook for 20 to 25 minutes, or until the rice is done and the liquid is gone.
5. Add pepper and salt to taste.
6. Before serving, sprinkle with chopped green onions.

MEDITERRANEAN CHICKPEA DELIGHT:

Ingredients:

- 2 cans (15 oz each) of chickpeas, drained and rinsed
- 1 cucumber, diced
- 1 cup cherry tomatoes, halved

- 1/2 red onion, finely chopped
- 1/2 cup Kalamata olives, sliced
- 1/2 cup feta cheese, crumbled
- 3 tablespoons olive oil
- 2 tablespoons red wine vinegar
- 1 teaspoon dried oregano
- Salt and pepper to taste

Instructions:

1. Put chickpeas, cucumber, cherry tomatoes, red onion, olives, and feta cheese in a big bowl.
2. Mix olive oil, red wine vinegar, dried oregano, salt, and pepper in a small bowl with a whisk.
3. Add the sauce to the chickpea mix and mix it all by tossing.
4. Serve cold.

SPANISH PAELLA PLEASER:

Ingredients:

- 1 pound chicken thighs, boneless and skinless, cut into chunks
- 1/2 pound chorizo sausage, sliced
- 1 onion, finely chopped
- 1 red bell pepper, sliced
- 1 yellow bell pepper, sliced
- 2 cups Arborio rice
- 4 cups chicken broth
- 1 can (14 oz) diced tomatoes
- 1 teaspoon smoked paprika
- 1 teaspoon saffron threads (optional)
- Salt and pepper to taste

- Lemon wedges for serving

Instructions:

1. With the heat on medium, brown the chicken thighs and chorizo in a big pan or skillet.
2. Cut up some onion and bell pepper and add them. Cook the veggies until they get soft.
3. Add the chopped tomatoes, smoked paprika, saffron threads (if using), salt, and pepper, and mix them in.
4. Put in the chicken soup and raise the heat. Put a lid on top and cook for 20 to 25 minutes or until the rice is soft and the liquid is gone.
5. Put lemon wedges on the side and serve.

MAPLE GLAZED BRUSSELS SPROUTS AND BACON:

Ingredients:

- 1 lb Brussels sprouts, trimmed and halved
- 4 slices bacon, chopped
- 2 tablespoons maple syrup
- 2 tablespoons olive oil
- Salt and pepper to taste

Instructions:

1. Warm the oven up to 200°C/400°F.
2. Add Brussels sprouts to a big bowl and season with salt and pepper.
3. Place Brussels sprouts in a single layer on a baking sheet.
4. Put chopped bacon on top of the Brussels sprouts.
5. After the oven is hot, roast the Brussels sprouts for 20 to 25 minutes or until golden brown and crispy.

6. Pour maple syrup over the bacon and roasted Brussels sprouts, then toss to coat everything.
7. Please put it back in the oven for five more minutes.
8. Enjoy while hot!

CAPRESE CHICKEN SKILLET:

Ingredients:

- 4 boneless, skinless chicken breasts
- Salt and pepper to taste
- 1 tablespoon olive oil
- 1 cup cherry tomatoes, halved
- 1 cup fresh mozzarella, sliced
- 1/4 cup fresh basil, chopped
- Balsamic glaze for drizzling

Instructions:

1. Add salt and pepper to the chicken breasts.
2. In a pan, heat the olive oil over medium-high heat.
3. Chicken breasts should be cooked on each side for 7 to 8 minutes or until fully cooked.
4. Put cherry tomatoes, mozzarella pieces, and fresh basil on each chicken breast.
5. Put the lid on the pan and cook for another two to three minutes or until the cheese melts.
6. Add the vinegar glaze right before serving.
7. Enjoy while hot!

LEMON GARLIC BUTTER SHRIMP:

Ingredients:

- 1 lb large shrimp, peeled and deveined
- 3 tablespoons butter

- 4 cloves garlic, minced
- 1 lemon, juiced
- Salt and pepper to taste
- 2 tablespoons fresh parsley, chopped

Instructions:

1. Melt the butter in a big pan over medium-low heat.
2. Add chopped garlic and cook until the garlic smells good.
3. Put the shrimp in the pan and cook them for two to three minutes on each side or until they turn pink.
4. Add salt and pepper to the shrimp after you squeeze lemon juice over them.
5. Place small pieces of parsley on top of the shrimp.
6. Add everything to the shrimp and toss it all together.
7. Enjoy while hot!

THAI BASIL BEEF STIR-FRY:

Ingredients:

- 1 lb flank steak, thinly sliced
- 2 tablespoons soy sauce
- 1 tablespoon oyster sauce
- 1 tablespoon fish sauce
- 1 tablespoon sugar
- 2 tablespoons vegetable oil
- 4 cloves garlic, minced
- 1 red chilli, sliced
- 1 cup fresh basil leaves

Instructions:

1. Mix sugar, oyster, fish, and soy sauce

in a bowl. Put away.

2. Heat the vegetable oil over a wok or big skillet over high heat.
3. Dice the flank steak and add it to the pan. Cook the meat in a stir-fry until it turns brown.
4. Add the sauce mix to the meat and mix it all.
5. Slice the red pepper and add the fresh basil leaves to the wok. Stir-fry for one to two more minutes.
6. Take it off the heat and put it on top of the rice.
7. Have fun with your Thai Basil Beef Stir-fry!

RANCH CHICKEN AND VEGGIE BAKE:

Ingredients:

- 4 boneless, skinless chicken breasts
- 1 cup cherry tomatoes, halved
- 1 cup baby potatoes, halved
- 1 cup baby carrots
- 1 bell pepper, sliced
- 1 zucchini, sliced
- 1/2 cup ranch dressing
- 1 tablespoon olive oil
- 1 teaspoon garlic powder
- 1 teaspoon onion powder
- Salt and pepper to taste
- Fresh parsley for garnish (optional)

Instructions:

1. Warm the oven up to 190°C (375°F).
2. Mix the chicken breasts, cherry tomatoes, baby carrots, bell peppers, and zucchini in a big bowl.
3. Mix the
4. olive oil, garlic powder, onion powder, salt, and pepper in a small bowl.

5. Cover the chicken and vegetables with the ranch sauce mixture by pouring it over them.
6. Put the mixture in a baking dish.
7. Put the pan in a hot oven and bake for 25 to 30 minutes until the chicken is done and the vegetables are soft.
8. If you want, you can add fresh parsley as a garnish before serving.

SWEET POTATO HASH HARMONY:

Ingredients:

- 2 large sweet potatoes, peeled and diced
- 1 onion, finely chopped
- 1 red bell pepper, diced
- 1 green bell pepper, diced
- 2 tablespoons olive oil
- 1 teaspoon smoked paprika
- 1/2 teaspoon garlic powder
- Salt and pepper to taste
- Fresh cilantro for garnish (optional)

Instructions:

1. Warm up a big pan with olive oil over medium-low heat.
2. Please put in the chopped onion and cook it until it turns clear.
3. Put red and green bell peppers, sweet potatoes, and onions in the pan.
4. Salt, pepper, and smoked paprika can season the food.
5. It will take about 15 to 20 minutes of cooking, stirring occasionally until the sweet potatoes are soft and slightly crispy.
6. If you want, add fresh cilantro as a garnish before serving.

BBQ PULLED PORK PARADISE:

Ingredients:

- 2 pounds pork shoulder, trimmed and cut into chunks
- 1 cup barbecue sauce
- 1 onion, finely chopped
- 2 cloves garlic, minced
- 1 teaspoon smoked paprika
- 1 teaspoon cumin
- Salt and pepper to taste
- Burger buns for serving

Instructions:

1. Put the pork shoulder pieces in a slow cooker.
2. BBQ sauce, chopped onion, sliced garlic, cumin, salt, and pepper should all be mixed in a bowl.
3. Cover every piece of pork with sauce as you pour it over it.
4. Low-key for 6 to 8 hours or until the pork is soft and easy to cut.
5. Using two forks, shred the pork, then mix it with the rest of the sauce.
6. Toast rolls and put the pulled pork on them.

RATATOUILLE RUSTIC DELIGHT:

Ingredients:

- 1 eggplant, diced
- 2 zucchinis, sliced
- 1 bell pepper, diced
- 1 onion, finely chopped
- 2 cloves garlic, minced
- 1 can (14 oz) diced tomatoes

- 2 tablespoons tomato paste
- 1 teaspoon dried thyme
- 1 teaspoon dried rosemary
- Salt and pepper to taste
- Olive oil for cooking

Instructions:

1. Warm up a big pan with olive oil over medium-low heat.
2. Put in the crushed garlic and chopped onion and cook until the onion is soft.
3. Dice the zucchini, eggplant, and bell pepper and add them to the pan. Keep cooking until the veggies get soft.
4. The tomato paste, dried thyme, rosemary, salt, and pepper should all be mixed in now.
5. Cover and cook for 20 to 25 minutes, stirring now and then.
6. Serve the ratatouille hot after the veggies are soft.

TERIYAKI QUINOA SKILLET:

Ingredients:

- 1 cup quinoa
- 2 cups water or vegetable broth
- 1 cup broccoli florets
- 1 bell pepper, sliced
- 1 carrot, sliced
- 1 cup snap peas, trimmed
- 1/2 cup teriyaki sauce
- 2 tablespoons soy sauce
- 1 tablespoon sesame oil
- 2 tablespoons vegetable oil
- 2 green onions, chopped
- Sesame seeds for garnish (optional)

Instructions:

1. Run cold water over the quinoa to clean it. Put the quinoa and water or vegetable broth in a medium pot. Bring to a boil, turn down the heat, cover, and let it simmer for 15 to 20 minutes, or until the quinoa is done and the water dries.
2. Warm the vegetable oil in a big pan or wok over medium-high heat. Put in the snap peas, bell pepper, carrot, and broccoli. Stir-fry the vegetables for 5 to 7 minutes or until they are soft but crisp.
3. Put the cooked quinoa in the pan with the veggies. Add the mix of soy sauce, teriyaki sauce, and olive oil. Mix everything well and cover it all equally. Add two to three more minutes of cooking time until everything is hot.
4. If you want, you can add chopped green onions and sesame seeds as a garnish. Serve right away.

PESTO PASTA PRIMAVERA:

Ingredients:

- 8 oz (about 225g) pasta of your choice
- 1 cup cherry tomatoes, halved
- 1 zucchini, thinly sliced
- 1 yellow squash, thinly sliced
- 1 bell pepper, thinly sliced
- 1/2 cup green beans, trimmed and cut into bite-sized pieces
- 1/2 cup fresh or frozen peas
- 1/2 cup pesto sauce (store-bought or homemade)
- Salt and pepper to taste
- Grated Parmesan cheese for serving (optional)

Instructions:

1. Follow the directions on the package to cook the pasta. Remove the water and set it aside.
2. Blanch the peas and green beans in a big pot of boiling water for two to three minutes until they are bright green and soft. Remove the water and set it aside.
3. Set a big pan on medium heat and add a little olive oil. Put in the peas, zucchini, yellow squash, bell pepper, small tomatoes, green beans that have been blanched, and zucchini. For 5 to 7 minutes, or until the vegetables are soft but bright, sauté them.
4. The pesto sauce and cooked pasta should be added to the pan. Add the pasta and veggies and toss them all together until the pesto runs over them. Add pepper and salt to taste.
5. If you want, you can sprinkle chopped Parmesan cheese on top of the hot Pesto Pasta Primavera.

VEGETARIAN VIBE:

LENTIL AND VEGETABLE CURRY:

Ingredients:

- 1 cup dried lentils
- 1 large onion, diced
- 2 cloves garlic, minced
- 1 can (14 oz) diced tomatoes
- 1 can (14 oz) coconut milk
- 2 cups mixed vegetables (carrots, peas, bell peppers, etc.)
- 2 tablespoons curry powder
- 1 teaspoon ground cumin
- 1 teaspoon ground coriander
- Salt and pepper to taste
- Fresh cilantro for garnish

Instructions:

1. Put the beans aside after running them under cold water.
2. Dice the onion and garlic in a big pot until they get soft.
3. Put the chopped tomatoes, coconut milk, mixed veggies, curry powder, cumin, and coriander in the pot along with the lentils. Mix well.
4. Add pepper and salt to taste. Turn down the heat and let the curry cook for twenty to twenty-five minutes or until the lentils are soft.
5. You can serve the lentil and vegetable soup with naan bread or rice. Top it off with fresh cilantro.

BUTTERNUT SQUASH RISOTTO RADIANCE:

Ingredients:

- 1 cup Arborio rice
- 2 cups butternut squash, diced
- 1 onion, finely chopped
- 2 cloves garlic, minced
- 4 cups vegetable broth, heated
- 1/2 cup dry white wine
- 1/2 cup Parmesan cheese, grated
- 2 tablespoons olive oil
- Salt and pepper to taste
- Fresh sage leaves for garnish

Instructions:

1. Set olive oil on medium heat in a big pan. Sauté the garlic and onions until they get soft.
2. Add the Arborio rice and mix it in to cover it in oil.
3. While cooking, add the white wine and let it soak in mostly.

4. Add hot vegetable broth one ladle at a time while turning often. Before adding the next spoonful, let the first one soak in.
5. Put in the diced butternut squash when the rice is almost done cooking.
6. It's important to keep adding broth until the rice and butternut squash are soft and smooth.
7. Season with salt and pepper, add the Parmesan cheese and top with fresh sage leaves.

CHICKPEA AND SPINACH STUFFED PEPPERS:

Ingredients:

- 4 large bell peppers, halved and seeds removed
- 1 can (15 oz) chickpeas, drained and rinsed
- 2 cups fresh spinach, chopped
- 1 cup cooked quinoa
- 1 onion, diced
- 2 cloves garlic, minced
- 1 teaspoon ground cumin
- 1 teaspoon paprika
- Salt and pepper to taste
- Olive oil for cooking
- 1 cup tomato sauce for topping
- Grated cheese for topping (optional)

Instructions:

1. Warm the oven up to 190°C (375°F).
2. Put the chopped garlic and diced onion in a pan with olive oil and cook them until they get soft.
3. Add cooked rice, chopped spinach, ground cumin, paprika, salt, and pepper to the pan. Make the spinach wilt.

4. Put the bean and spinach mixture inside the bell peppers that have been cut in half.
5. Stuff the peppers and put them in a baking dish. Add tomato sauce and chopped cheese, if you want, on top of each one.
6. Place paper over the baking dish and bake for 25 to 30 minutes or until the peppers are soft.
7. Do not cool the stuffed peppers down.

QUINOA AND BLACK BEAN BUDDHA BOWL:

Ingredients:

- 1 cup quinoa, rinsed
- 2 cups black beans, cooked and drained
- 1 cup cherry tomatoes, halved
- 1 cucumber, diced
- 1 avocado, sliced
- 1 cup shredded carrots
- 1/4 cup chopped fresh cilantro
- 2 tablespoons olive oil
- 1 tablespoon lime juice
- 1 teaspoon ground cumin
- Salt and pepper to taste

Instructions:

1. Follow the directions on the package to cook the quinoa.
2. Cooked quinoa, black beans, cucumber, avocado, shredded carrots, and cilantro should all be put in a big bowl together.
3. Salt and pepper should be mixed with olive oil, lime juice, ground cumin, and salt in a small bowl.
4. Add the dressing to the rice and black bean mix and mix it in. Carefully toss to mix.

5. You can serve the Buddha bowl immediately or put it in the fridge for later use.

CAULIFLOWER ALFREDO PASTA:

Ingredients:

- 1 medium cauliflower, chopped
- 2 cloves garlic, minced
- 1 cup vegetable broth
- 1 cup unsweetened almond milk
- 1/2 cup nutritional yeast
- 2 tablespoons olive oil
- Salt and pepper to taste
- 12 oz fettuccine pasta, cooked according to package instructions
- Fresh parsley for garnish (optional)

Instructions:

1. You can boil or steam the cauliflower until it's soft.
2. Put the garlic, veggie broth, almond milk, nutritional yeast, olive oil, salt, and pepper in a blender. Mix until it's creamy and smooth.
3. Put the cauliflower Alfredo sauce in a large pan and heat it over medium-sized heat.
4. When the pasta is done, add it to the pan and toss it around so that all of the sauce covers it.
5. If you want, you can serve it hot with fresh parsley on top.

SWEET POTATO AND KALE HASH:

Ingredients:

- 2 sweet potatoes, peeled and diced
- 1 bunch kale, stems removed and leaves chopped

- 1 onion, diced
- 2 cloves garlic, minced
- 2 tablespoons olive oil
- Salt and pepper to taste
- 1 teaspoon paprika
- 1/2 teaspoon cumin

INSTRUCTIONS:

1. Warm up the olive oil in a big pan over medium-low heat.
2. Toss in the sweet potatoes and cook them until they start to brown and get soft.
3. Put chopped garlic and diced onion in the pan. Sauté until the onion turns clear.
4. Cook until the kale wilts after adding the chopped kale.
5. Put in some cumin, salt, pepper, and paprika to taste. Add everything to the bowl and mix it well.
6. Cook the kale and sweet potatoes until they are soft; the kale is how you like it.
7. As a major dish or a side dish, serve hot.

ZUCCHINI NOODLE STIR-FRY:

Ingredients:

- 4 medium zucchinis, spiralized into noodles
- 1 bell pepper, thinly sliced
- 1 carrot, julienned
- 1 cup broccoli florets
- 2 tablespoons soy sauce
- 1 tablespoon sesame oil
- 1 tablespoon olive oil
- 2 cloves garlic, minced
- 1 teaspoon grated ginger

- Sesame seeds for garnish (optional)
- Green onions, chopped, for garnish (optional)

Instructions:

1. Heat the olive oil over medium-high heat in a big pan or wok.
2. Grate the ginger and chop the garlic. Sauté for one to two minutes until the food smells good.
3. Put cabbage, carrot, and bell pepper in the pan. Stir-fry the veggies until they are crisp and soft.
4. Toss the noodles in with the sauce and cook for two to three minutes.
5. Mix the soy sauce and sesame oil with the meat and veggies. Toss until everything is covered.
6. If you want, you can add sesame seeds and chopped green onions as a garnish.
7. Serve right away.

EGGPLANT PARMESAN ELEGANCE

Ingredients:

- 2 large eggplants, sliced into 1/2-inch rounds
- 2 cups marinara sauce
- 1 cup breadcrumbs (gluten-free if needed)
- 1 cup grated Parmesan cheese (vegan option if desired)
- 2 cups shredded mozzarella cheese (vegan option if desired)
- 2 tablespoons olive oil
- Salt and pepper to taste
- Fresh basil for garnish (optional)

Instructions:

1. Warm the oven up to 190°C (375°F).

2. Add salt and pepper to the eggplant pieces and brush both sides with olive oil.
3. Cover each slice of eggplant with breadcrumbs and press them down onto the eggplant.
4. Butter the eggplant slices and put them on a baking sheet. Bake for 20 to 25 minutes or until they turn golden brown.
5. Spoon a little tomato sauce into a baking dish. Spread out some baked eggplant slices on top.
6. On top of the eggplant, sprinkle Parmesan and mozzarella cheese. Please do it again, and this time, add a layer of cheese on top.
7. Please put it in the oven and bake for 25 to 30 minutes or until the cheese melts and bubbles.
8. If you want, add fresh basil as a garnish.
9. Let it cool down for a while before you serve it.

GREEK SALAD STUFFED PITA POCKETS:

Ingredients:

- 2 cups cherry tomatoes, halved
- 1 cucumber, diced
- 1 bell pepper, diced
- 1 red onion, finely chopped
- 1 cup Kalamata olives, pitted and sliced
- 1 cup feta cheese, crumbled
- 1/4 cup fresh parsley, chopped
- 4 whole wheat pita pockets

Instructions:

1. Add the cucumber, bell pepper, red onion, olives, feta cheese, and cherry tomatoes to a big bowl.

2. Add the olive oil and toss everything together. Put in some new parsley and mix it in again.
3. Cut the bread pockets in half and open each one slowly.
4. Fill the pita holes with the Greek salad mix.
5. Serve your Greek Salad Stuffed Pita Pockets right away, and enjoy them!

SPINACH AND MUSHROOM QUESADILLA:

Ingredients:

- 8 large flour tortillas
- 2 cups fresh spinach, chopped
- 2 cups mushrooms, sliced
- 2 cups shredded mozzarella cheese
- 1 tablespoon olive oil
- Salt and pepper to taste

Instructions:

1. Add olive oil to a pan and cook mushrooms and spinach until the spinach wilts. Add pepper and salt.
2. Put a tortilla in a pan that's on medium heat.
3. Put some cheese on top of half of the bread.
4. Place some of the spinach and mushrooms cooked on top of the cheese.
5. To make a half-moon form, fold the tortilla in half.
6. Ensure the cheese melts and both sides of the tortilla turn golden brown.
7. Please do it again with the rest of the filling and tortillas.
8. Spread the Spinach and Mushroom Quesadillas on a plate and serve them hot.

ROASTED VEGETABLE LASAGNA LOVE:

Ingredients:

- 9 lasagna noodles, cooked according to package instructions
- 3 cups mixed roasted vegetables (e.g., zucchini, bell peppers, eggplant)
- 2 cups ricotta cheese
- 2 cups shredded mozzarella cheese
- 2 cups marinara sauce
- 1/2 cup grated Parmesan cheese
- Fresh basil for garnish

Instructions:

1. Warm the oven up to 190°C (375°F).
2. Spoon a little tomato sauce into a baking dish.
3. On top of the sauce, put three lasagna noodles.
4. Cover half of the noodles with ricotta cheese. Then, cover half of the noodles with roasted veggies and mozzarella cheese.
5. Layer it again, ending with a layer of mozzarella and some Parmesan cheese.
6. Toast it for 25 to 30 minutes or until it turns brown and bubbly.
7. While it's still warm, add some fresh basil, cut it up, and serve.

FALAFEL FEAST WITH TAHINI SAUCE:

Ingredients:

- 2 cans (15 oz each) of chickpeas, drained and rinsed
- 1 small onion, chopped
- 3 cloves garlic, minced
- 1 cup fresh parsley, chopped
- 1 teaspoon ground cumin
- 1 teaspoon ground coriander

- 1/2 teaspoon cayenne pepper
- Salt and pepper to taste
- 1/4 cup all-purpose flour
- Vegetable oil for frying

Tahini Sauce:

- 1/2 cup tahini
- 2 tablespoons lemon juice
- 2 tablespoons water
- 2 tablespoons olive oil
- 1 clove garlic, minced
- Salt to taste

Instructions:

1. Put the chickpeas, onion, garlic, parsley, cumin, coriander, cayenne, salt, and pepper in a food processor and blend them. Pulse until nothing is left out.
2. Add the flour and mix it in after moving the batter to a bowl.
3. Then, use vegetable oil to fry the patties until they are golden brown on both sides.
4. Mix the tahini sauce in a bowl by whisking the tahini, lemon juice, water, olive oil, garlic, and salt.
5. Throw the falafel pieces on the plate and top them with the tahini sauce. Enjoy your Falafel Feast!

TOMATO BASIL MOZZARELLA CAPRESE:

Ingredients:

- Fresh tomatoes (sliced)
- Fresh mozzarella cheese (sliced)
- Fresh basil leaves

- Extra virgin olive oil
- Balsamic glaze
- Salt and pepper to taste

Instructions:

1. Arrange tomato, mozzarella, and basil slices in a circle on a serving plate.
2. Add extra virgin olive oil and balsamic glaze on top.
3. Add pepper and salt to taste.
4. As a cool starter or side dish, serve right away.

BLACK BEAN AND CORN ENCHILADAS:

Ingredients:

- 1 can black beans, drained and rinsed
- 1 cup corn kernels (fresh or frozen)
- 1 cup shredded cheddar cheese
- 1 cup enchilada sauce
- 8 small flour tortillas
- Optional toppings: diced tomatoes, chopped green onions, sour cream, guacamole

Instructions:

1. Warm the oven up to 190°C (375°F).
2. Put half of the cheese, the corn, and the black beans in a bowl.
3. Put some of the bean and corn mix on each tortilla, then roll them up.
4. Put the tortillas that have been rolled into a baking dish.
5. Cover it with enchilada sauce and top it with the rest of the cheese.
6. Please put it in the oven and bake for twenty minutes or until the cheese melts and bubbles.

7. Top with your best things.

BROCCOLI CHEDDAR STUFFED PORTOBELLOS:

Ingredients:

- Portobello mushrooms (cleaned and stems removed)
- 1 cup broccoli florets, steamed
- 1 cup shredded cheddar cheese
- Olive oil
- Salt and pepper to taste

Instructions:

1. Warm the oven up to 190°C (375°F).
2. Put the portobello mushrooms on a baking sheet and brush them with olive oil.
3. You can put steamed broccoli in each mushroom and then top it with chopped cheddar cheese.
4. Add pepper and salt.
5. Please put it in the oven and bake for 15 to 20 minutes until the cheese melts and the mushrooms soften.
6. You can eat it as a side meal or a vegetarian main course.

SPINACH AND ARTICHOKE QUICHE:

Ingredients:

- 1 pie crust (store-bought or homemade)
- 1 cup fresh spinach, chopped
- 1 can artichoke hearts, drained and chopped
- 1 cup shredded Swiss or Gruyere cheese
- 4 large eggs
- 1 cup milk or half-and-half
- Salt and pepper to taste

Instructions:

1. Warm the oven up to 190°C (375°F).
2. Put the pie crust in a pie plate.
3. Cover the bread with chopped artichoke hearts and spinach.
4. Add eggs, milk, salt, and pepper to a bowl and mix them using a whisk. Please put it on top of the artichokes and spinach.
5. Add some shreds of cheese on top.
6. Put the quiche in the oven and bake for 30 to 35 minutes or until it's set and golden brown.
7. Let it cool down for a while before cutting it.

MUSHROOM WELLINGTON WONDER:

Ingredients:

- 1 sheet of puff pastry, thawed
- 2 cups of mushrooms, finely chopped (a combination of button mushrooms and portobello mushrooms works well)
- 1 onion, finely chopped
- 2 cloves of garlic, minced
- 1 tablespoon olive oil
- 1 teaspoon thyme, chopped
- Salt and pepper to taste
- 1/2 cup breadcrumbs
- 1/2 cup vegan cream cheese
- Dijon mustard for brushing

Instructions:

1. Warm the oven up to 200°C (400°F).

2. Put olive oil in a pan and heat it over medium-low heat. Chopped onions and garlic should be added and cooked until soft.
3. Put chopped mushrooms in the pan and cook them until they lose their water.
4. Add salt, pepper, and thyme to taste. Add the breadcrumbs to soak up any extra liquid.
5. Take it off the heat and let it cool down. Add the vegan cream cheese after it has cooled down.
6. On a greased surface, roll out the puff pastry sheet. Add a layer of Dijon mustard to the dough.
7. Leave some space around the sides of the puff pastry as you spoon the mushroom mixture.
8. Put the mushroom filling inside the puff pastry and carefully fold and seal it.
9. It should be placed on a baking sheet seam side down. Add some olive oil to the top.
10. Put the dough in an oven that has already been cooked for 25 to 30 minutes or until it turns golden brown.
11. Let it cool down for a while before cutting it. Serve and have fun!

THAI PEANUT ZOODLES ZING:

Ingredients:

- 4 medium zucchinis, spiralized into noodles (zoodles)
- 1 cup shredded carrots
- 1 red bell pepper, thinly sliced
- 1 cup snap peas, thinly sliced
- 1/2 cup chopped peanuts
- Fresh cilantro for garnish

For the Peanut Sauce:

- 1/3 cup peanut butter
- 3 tablespoons soy sauce
- 2 tablespoons lime juice
- 2 tablespoons rice vinegar
- 1 tablespoon sesame oil
- 1 tablespoon maple syrup
- 1 teaspoon ginger, grated
- 1 clove garlic, minced
- 1/4 teaspoon red pepper flakes (optional)

Instructions:

1. Sliced bell pepper, snap peas, spiralized zucchini, and shredded carrots should all be together in a big bowl.
2. Mix the peanut sauce ingredients in a different bowl with a whisk until smooth.
3. Add the peanut sauce to the vegetables and toss them around until they are well-covered.
4. Before serving, top with chopped peanuts and fresh parsley.
5. Let it sit at room temperature or in the fridge.

GLOBAL FLAVORS IN YOUR SKILLET:

MOROCCAN CHICKEN TAGINE:

Ingredients:

- 1.5 lbs (700g) chicken, cut into pieces
- 2 tablespoons olive oil
- 1 onion, finely chopped
- 2 cloves garlic, minced
- 1 teaspoon ground cumin

- 1 teaspoon ground coriander
- 1 teaspoon ground cinnamon
- 1 teaspoon paprika
- 1/2 teaspoon turmeric
- Salt and pepper to taste
- 1 cup chicken broth
- 1 cup diced tomatoes
- 1/2 cup dried apricots, chopped
- 1/4 cup sliced almonds
- Fresh cilantro for garnish

Instructions:

1. Heat the olive oil over medium-low heat in a big pot or tagine.
2. Put the chicken pieces in and cook them all over. Take it out and set it aside.
3. Cook the onions in the same pot until they get soft. Put in the garlic and cook for one more minute.
4. Add the cinnamon, paprika, turmeric, salt, and pepper and mix them in.
5. Put the chicken back in the pot. Put in chicken stock, tomato chunks, and dried apricots. Bring to a low boil.
6. Place the dish on a low heat and cover it. Cook for 45 to 60 minutes or until the chicken is fully cooked and soft.
7. Before serving, top with sliced almonds and fresh parsley.

BRAZILIAN FEIJOADA FIESTA:

Ingredients:

- 1 lb (450g) black beans, soaked overnight
- 1 lb (450g) smoked sausage, sliced
- 1 lb (450g) pork shoulder, cubed
- 1/2 lb (225g) bacon, chopped

- 1 onion, chopped
- 4 cloves garlic, minced
- 2 bay leaves
- 1 orange, sliced
- Salt and pepper to taste
- Cooked rice for serving

Instructions:

1. Take black beans that have been soaked and put them in a big pot. Add smoked sausage, pork shoulder, bacon, onion, garlic, and bay leaves.
2. Bring the food to a boil and add enough water to cover it.
3. Lower the heat, cover, and let the beans cook for two to three hours or until soft.
4. Add pepper and salt to taste.
5. Serve with rice and orange pieces on top.

JAPANESE TERIYAKI BOWL:

Ingredients:

- 1 lb (450g) boneless chicken thighs, sliced
- 1/2 cup soy sauce
- 1/4 cup mirin
- 2 tablespoons sake or dry white wine
- 2 tablespoons sugar
- 1 tablespoon vegetable oil
- 2 cups cooked rice
- Steamed broccoli, sliced green onions, and sesame seeds for garnish

Instructions:

1. Mix the soy sauce, mirin, sake, and sugar in a bowl to make the teriyaki sauce.

2. In a pan, heat vegetable oil over medium-high heat.
3. Please put in the chicken slices and cook until they turn brown.
4. Put the chicken in the teriyaki sauce and cook until it gets thick.
5. Put the teriyaki chicken on top of the cooked rice. Add steamed broccoli, green onions, and sesame seeds to the rice.

SPANISH CHORIZO PAELLA:

Ingredients:

- 1 lb (450g) chicken thighs, cut into pieces
- 1/2 lb (225g) Spanish chorizo, sliced
- 1 onion, finely chopped
- 2 bell peppers, diced
- 2 cups Arborio rice
- 4 cups chicken broth
- 1 teaspoon saffron threads
- 1 teaspoon smoked paprika
- Salt and pepper to taste
- 1 cup frozen peas
- Lemon wedges for serving

Instructions:

1. While the pan is on medium-high heat, cook the chicken and chorizo

2. Please put in the chopped onion and bell peppers and cook them until they get soft.
3. Add the smoked paprika, Arborio rice, and saffron threads and mix them in.

4. Set the pot on low heat and add the chicken broth. Season with salt and pepper.
5. Turn down the heat and leave the lid off for 15 to 20 minutes, or until the rice is soft and the liquid is gone.
6. Add the frozen peas to the paella and cook for five more minutes.
7. Comes with lemon pieces.

INDIAN BUTTER CHICKEN DELIGHT:

Ingredients:

- 1.5 lbs boneless, skinless chicken thighs cut into bite-sized pieces
- 1 cup plain yogurt
- 2 tablespoons garam masala
- 1 tablespoon ground turmeric
- 1 tablespoon ground cumin
- 2 teaspoons chilli powder
- 1 tablespoon ginger, minced
- 1 tablespoon garlic, minced
- 1 cup tomato puree
- 1 cup heavy cream
- 4 tablespoons butter
- Salt to taste
- Fresh cilantro for garnish

Instructions:

1. Garam masala, turmeric, cumin, chilli powder, ginger, and garlic should all be mixed in a bowl.
2. Ensure the chicken pieces are well covered when adding them to the marinate. For at least 30 minutes, let it sit.
3. In a pan, melt butter. Add the chicken that has been marinating and cook until it turns brown.

4. After you add the tomato sauce, cook for 5 to 7 minutes.
5. Add the heavy cream, stir it in, and let it cook while you watch.
6. Add salt to taste, and then top with fresh cilantro.

THAI GREEN CURRY TRIUMPH:

Ingredients:

- 1 lb boneless chicken, thinly sliced
- 1 can (14 oz) coconut milk
- 2 tablespoons green curry paste
- 1 tablespoon fish sauce
- 1 tablespoon soy sauce
- 1 tablespoon brown sugar
- 1 bell pepper, sliced
- 1 zucchini, sliced
- Fresh basil leaves for garnish
- Cooked jasmine rice

Instructions:

1. In a pan, heat the coconut milk over medium-low heat.
2. Stir in the green curry paste until it smells good.
3. Fish sauce, soy sauce, and brown sugar should be added. Make sure the chicken is fully cooked.
4. Put in the zucchini and bell pepper. Simmer until the veggies are soft.
5. Please put it on cooked jasmine rice and add fresh basil leaves.

MEXICAN STREET CORN SKILLET:

Ingredients:

- 4 cups corn kernels (fresh or frozen)

- 1/2 cup mayonnaise
- 1/2 cup sour cream
- 1 cup cotija cheese, crumbled
- 1 teaspoon chilli powder
- 1/4 cup fresh cilantro, chopped
- Lime wedges for serving

Instructions:

1. Put the corn in a pan over medium-low heat and cook it until it gets charred.
2. Mix sour cream, mayonnaise, and half of the cotija cheese in a bowl.
3. Mix the mayo mixture into the pan by stirring it in well.
4. Cover the corn with the chilli sauce, the rest of the cotija cheese, and the cilantro.
5. Put lime wedges on the side and serve.

ITALIAN SAUSAGE AND PEPPERS:

Ingredients:

- 1 lb Italian sausage, sliced
- 2 bell peppers, sliced
- 1 onion, sliced
- 2 cloves garlic, minced
- 1 can (14 oz) crushed tomatoes
- 1 teaspoon dried oregano
- 1 teaspoon dried basil
- Salt and pepper to taste
- Olive oil for cooking
- Fresh parsley for garnish

Instructions:

1. In a pan, heat the olive oil. Add the sausage and cook it until it turns brown.
2. Put in the garlic, onions, and bell peppers. Cook the veggies until they get soft.
3. Add the oregano, basil, salt, pepper, and crushed tomatoes. Let it cook for 15 to 20 minutes.
4. Before serving, sprinkle with fresh parsley.

KOREAN BBQ BEEF STIR-FRY:

Ingredients:

- 1 lb (450g) thinly sliced beef (ribeye or sirloin)
- 3 tablespoons soy sauce
- 2 tablespoons brown sugar
- 1 tablespoon sesame oil
- 3 cloves garlic, minced
- 1 teaspoon ginger, grated
- 2 tablespoons vegetable oil
- 1 onion, thinly sliced
- 1 bell pepper, thinly sliced
- 1 carrot, julienned
- 4 green onions, chopped
- Sesame seeds for garnish

Instructions:

1. Mix soy sauce, brown sugar, olive oil, garlic, and ginger in a bowl to make the sauce.
2. Put the meat in the mix and sit for at least 30 minutes.
3. Put oil from the vegetable pan or wok on medium-high heat.
4. The meat should be stir-fried until it turns brown and is fully cooked. Take it out of the pan.

5. The veggies should be stir-fried in the same pan until they are crisp-tender.
6. Mix everything well after you add the cooked beef back to the pan.
7. Put green onions and sesame seeds that have been chopped on top. Put on top of rice.

JAMAICAN JERK CHICKEN MEDLEY:

Ingredients:

- 4 chicken breasts, cut into strips
- 4 tablespoons Jamaican jerk seasoning
- 2 tablespoons olive oil
- 1 red bell pepper, sliced
- 1 yellow bell pepper, sliced
- 1 red onion, sliced
- 2 cups pineapple chunks
- Fresh cilantro for garnish

Instructions:

1. Jamaican jerk spice should be rubbed into the chicken strips for 30 minutes.
2. In a pan, heat the olive oil over medium-high heat.
3. Turn the chicken over and cook it all the way through until it's browned.
4. Put onions and bell pepper slices in the pan and cook until tender-crisp.
5. Add the pineapple chunks and stir them in. Cook for another two to three minutes.
6. Add fresh cilantro and serve with rice or your favourite side dish.

GREEK LEMON HERB SHRIMP:

Ingredients:

- 1 lb (450g) shrimp, peeled and deveined
- 3 tablespoons olive oil
- 3 cloves garlic, minced
- 1 teaspoon dried oregano
- 1 teaspoon dried thyme
- Zest of 1 lemon
- Juice of 1 lemon
- Salt and pepper to taste
- Feta cheese for garnish
- Fresh parsley for garnish

Instructions:

1. Add the garlic, oregano, thyme, lemon zest, lemon juice, salt, and pepper to a bowl. Then, add the shrimp. Allow it to sit for 15 to 20 minutes.
2. Set the pan on medium-high heat.
3. The shrimp should be cooked until they are pink and opaque.
4. Add fresh parsley and chopped feta cheese as a garnish.
5. You can eat it with toasted bread or rice.

PERUVIAN LOMO SALTADO ADVENTURE:

Ingredients:

- 1 lb (450g) beef sirloin, thinly sliced
- 3 tablespoons soy sauce
- 2 tablespoons red wine vinegar
- 1 tablespoon vegetable oil
- 1 red onion, sliced
- 2 tomatoes, sliced into wedges
- 1 bell pepper, sliced

- 3 cloves garlic, minced
- 1 teaspoon cumin
- Salt and pepper to taste
- Fresh cilantro for garnish
- French fries for serving

Instructions:

1. Put the sliced meat in a bowl and mix in the soy sauce and red wine vinegar.
2. Put oil from plants into a big pan or wok and heat it over high heat.
3. Fork-sear the meat that has been marinated and add it to the pan.
4. Slice the onion, bell pepper, and garlic and add them. Cook the veggies until they are almost soft.
5. Add the cumin and tomato pieces and mix well. Add two to three more minutes of cooking.
6. Add pepper and salt to taste.
7. Add fresh cilantro as a garnish.
8. Could you put it on top of French fries or rice?

LEBANESE FATTOUSH FRENZY:

Ingredients:

- 2 cups chopped romaine lettuce
- 1 cup chopped cucumber
- 1 cup chopped tomatoes
- 1 cup chopped radishes
- 1/2 cup chopped red onion
- 1/2 cup chopped fresh mint
- 1/4 cup chopped fresh parsley
- 1/4 cup extra virgin olive oil
- 2 tablespoons fresh lemon juice

- 1 teaspoon sumac
- Salt and pepper to taste
- 1 cup crispy pita chips (optional)

Instructions:

1. Put the lettuce, cucumber, tomatoes, radishes, red onion, mint, and parsley in a big bowl.
2. Mix the sumac, olive oil, lemon juice, salt, and pepper in a small bowl with a whisk.
3. Add the sauce to the salad and mix it all.
4. If you want, you can add the fried pita chips right before serving.

VIETNAMESE PHO FUSION:

Ingredients:

- 8 cups beef or vegetable broth
- 200g rice noodles
- 1 cup thinly sliced beef sirloin or tofu for a vegetarian option
- 1 onion, thinly sliced
- 2-inch piece of ginger, sliced
- 2-star anise
- 1 cinnamon stick
- 3 cloves
- 1 tablespoon soy sauce
- 1 tablespoon fish sauce (omit for vegetarian)
- Fresh bean sprouts, lime wedges, and fresh cilantro for garnish

Instructions:

1. Set the soup on low heat in a large pot.

2. Chop up the onion, ginger, star anise, cinnamon stick, and cloves, and add them to the soup.
3. Follow the directions on the package to cook the rice noodles.
4. Add soy sauce and fish sauce to the water to make it taste better.
5. Add the cooked noodles to bowls, then pour the hot soup.
6. Bean sprouts, lime pieces, and fresh cilantro should be served on the side.

CAJUN SHRIMP AND GRITS:

Ingredients:

- 1 cup stone-ground grits
- 1 pound large shrimp, peeled and deveined
- 1 tablespoon Cajun seasoning
- 1/2 cup diced andouille sausage
- 1 bell pepper, diced
- 1 onion, diced
- 2 cloves garlic, minced
- 1 cup chicken broth
- 1/2 cup heavy cream
- Salt and pepper to taste
- Chopped green onions for garnish

Instructions:

1. Follow the directions on the package to cook the grits.
2. Sprinkle Cajun spice on the shrimp.
3. Cook the andouille sausage in a pan until it turns brown. Then, add the onion, bell pepper, and garlic. Cook the veggies until they get soft.
4. Put shrimp in the pan and cook them until they turn pink.

5. Add the heavy cream and chicken broth, and let the sauce cook until thick.
6. Add salt and pepper, serve over grits, and top with green onions that have been chopped.

IRISH COLCANNON CELEBRATION:

Ingredients:

- 4 cups mashed potatoes
- 4 cups chopped kale or cabbage, blanched
- 1 cup chopped green onions
- 1/2 cup butter
- Salt and pepper to taste

Instructions:

1. Make potato mash.
2. Blanch the cabbage or kale in a different pot until it is soft.
3. Add chopped kale or cabbage to the mashed potatoes.
4. Put green onions in a pan and add butter. Cook them until they get soft.
5. Add the green onions and butter to the veggies and mashed potatoes.
6. Add pepper and salt, mix well, and serve.

TURKISH LAMB KOFTA:

Ingredients:

- 1 pound ground lamb
- 1 small onion, finely grated
- 2 cloves garlic, minced
- 1/4 cup fresh parsley, finely chopped
- 1 teaspoon ground cumin

- 1 teaspoon ground coriander
- 1 teaspoon smoked paprika
- Salt and pepper to taste
- Olive oil (for grilling or cooking)

Instructions:

1. Put minced garlic, chopped parsley, cumin, coriander, smoked paprika, salt, and pepper in a big bowl. Add the ground lamb and mix them all together.
2. Thoroughly mix the items until they are well blended. For this step, you can use your hands.
3. Shape the mixture into small, long sausage-like shapes to make the kofta shapes.
4. In a grill pan or on a grill, heat the olive oil.
5. Grill the lamb kofta until they are browned and fully cooked. To make sure they cook evenly, flip them over every so often.
6. Put the kofta in a pita with vegetables and your favourite sauce. You can also serve it with yoghurt.

CHINESE CASHEW CHICKEN:

Ingredients:

- 1 pound boneless, skinless chicken breasts cut into bite-sized pieces
- 1/2 cup cashews, unsalted
- 1 bell pepper, sliced
- 1 cup broccoli florets
- 3 tablespoons soy sauce
- 2 tablespoons oyster sauce
- 1 tablespoon hoisin sauce

- 1 tablespoon cornstarch
- 2 tablespoons vegetable oil
- 3 cloves garlic, minced
- 1 teaspoon ginger, minced
- Cooked rice for serving

Instructions:

1. Soy sauce, oyster sauce, hoisin sauce, and cornstarch should all be mixed in a small bowl. Put away.
2. Put oil from the vegetable pan or wok on medium-high heat.
3. When you add the chopped garlic and ginger, stir-fry for about 30 seconds or until the food smells good.
4. Put the chicken pieces in the wok and stir-fry until they are brown and fully cooked.
5. Slice the broccoli and bell pepper and add them to the wok. Stir-fry for a few more minutes until the veggies are soft but crisp.
6. Cover the chicken and veggies with the sauce. Mix everything well to cover it all.
7. Add the nuts and mix them in.
8. Add two to three more minutes of cooking until the sauce gets thick.
9. Put the chicken with cashews in China on top of cooked rice.

COMFORT FOOD CLASSICS:

CHICKEN POT PIE PERFECTION:

Ingredients:

- 1 pound boneless, skinless chicken breasts, cooked and shredded

- 2 cups frozen mixed vegetables (peas, carrots, corn, green beans)
- 1/3 cup butter
- 1/3 cup all-purpose flour
- 1/2 teaspoon salt
- 1/4 teaspoon black pepper
- 1/4 teaspoon celery seed
- 1/4 teaspoon onion powder
- 1/4 teaspoon garlic powder
- 1 3/4 cups chicken broth
- 2/3 cup milk
- 2 pre-made pie crusts

Instructions:

1. Warm the oven up to 425°F (220°C).
2. Melt the butter in a big pan over medium-low heat. Add the celery seed, onion powder, garlic powder, salt, and pepper, and mix them in until everything is well mixed.
3. Slowly whisk in the milk and chicken broth. Stir and cook the mixture some more until it gets thick.
4. Add the shredded chicken and mixed veggies to the pan and stir them in the creamy sauce until they are well covered.
5. Put one pie crust in a pie dish after rolling it out. Fill the crust with the chicken mix.
6. Before putting the second pie crust on top, roll it out. To seal the pie, cut and crimp the sides.
7. Make a few holes in the top crust to let the steam escape. Please put it in the oven for 30 to 35 minutes or until the top turns golden brown.

BEEF STROGANOFF SUPREME:

Ingredients:

- 1 pound beef sirloin or tenderloin, thinly sliced
- 2 tablespoons olive oil
- 1 onion, finely chopped
- 2 cloves garlic, minced
- 8 ounces mushrooms, sliced
- 2 tablespoons flour
- 1 cup beef broth
- 2 tablespoons Worcestershire sauce
- 1 teaspoon Dijon mustard
- 1/2 cup sour cream
- Salt and pepper to taste
- Cooked egg noodles or rice for serving

Instructions:

1. Warm up the olive oil in a big pan over medium-high heat. Please put in the chopped beef and cook it until it turns brown. Take the meat out of the pan and set it aside.
2. If you need to, add more oil to the same pan. Add the chopped onion and garlic and cook them until they get soft.
3. When you add the sliced mushrooms, cook them until they dry out and turn golden brown.
4. Add the flour to the veggies and mix them.
5. The meat broth, Worcestershire sauce, and Dijon mustard should be added slowly while whisking. Please bring it to a low boil and let it thicken.
6. Turn down the heat and add the cooked beef. Let it cook slowly for a few minutes until the beef is fully cooked.
7. Take it off the heat and add the sour cream. Add pepper and salt to taste.
8. Serve with egg noodles or rice that have been cooked.

MACARONI AND CHEESE MADNESS:

Ingredients:

- 8 ounces elbow macaroni
- 1/4 cup butter
- 1/4 cup all-purpose flour
- 1/2 teaspoon salt
- 1/4 teaspoon black pepper
- 1/4 teaspoon mustard powder
- 1/4 teaspoon garlic powder
- 2 cups milk
- 2 1/2 cups shredded sharp cheddar cheese

Instructions:

1. Follow the directions on the package to cook the pasta. Remove the water and set it aside.
2. Melt the butter over medium-low heat in a big saucepan. Mix well with the garlic powder, mustard powder, salt, pepper, and flour.
3. Whisk in the milk little by little. Stir and cook the mixture some more until it gets thick.
4. Turn down the heat and add the cheddar cheese shreds. Mix the sauce and cheese until it's smooth.
5. Mix the cooked pasta into the cheese sauce to cover it.
6. You can serve it hot or bake it in an oven set to 350°F (175°C) for 15 to 20 minutes if you'd rather.

CLASSIC MEATLOAF MAGIC:

Ingredients:

- 1 1/2 pounds ground beef
- 1 cup breadcrumbs
- 1/2 cup milk

- 1/4 cup ketchup
- 1/4 cup finely chopped onion
- 2 cloves garlic, minced
- 1 teaspoon Worcestershire sauce
- 1 teaspoon dried oregano
- 1/2 teaspoon salt
- 1/4 teaspoon black pepper
- 2 large eggs, beaten

Instructions:

1. Warm the oven up to 175°F (350°F).
2. Ground beef, breadcrumbs, milk, ketchup, chopped onion, minced garlic, Worcestershire sauce, oregano, salt, pepper, and beaten eggs should all be mixed in a big bowl.
3. Combine the parts until they are well mixed. To keep the meatloaf soft, use it sparingly.
4. Make a loaf from the dough and put it in a baking dish.
5. Bake for an hour or until the middle temperature hits 70°F (160°C).
6. Let the meatloaf cool down for a few minutes before cutting it.

CREAMY TOMATO BASIL SOUP:

Ingredients:

- 1 tablespoon olive oil
- 1 onion, chopped
- 2 cloves garlic, minced
- 2 cans (28 ounces each) of crushed tomatoes
- 1 can (14 ounces) diced tomatoes
- 4 cups vegetable or chicken broth
- 1 cup heavy cream
- Salt and pepper, to taste

- 1/4 cup fresh basil, chopped
- 1/2 cup grated Parmesan cheese (optional)

Instructions:

1. Set the olive oil in a big pot over medium-low heat. Please put in the chopped onion and cook it until it gets soft.
2. Add the minced garlic and cook for another one to two minutes, until the garlic smells good.
3. Add the water and the chopped and crushed tomatoes. Let the food cook for about 15 to 20 minutes after you bring it to a boil.
4. Blend the soup until it's smooth with an immersion mixer. Move the soup to a blender in batches if you don't have an immersion mixer.
5. Add the heavy cream, salt, and pepper, and mix them in. Let it cook for another 10 minutes.
6. Mix in the basil leaves. Add chopped Parmesan cheese on top if you want to before serving.

CHICKEN AND DUMPLINGS DREAM:

Ingredients:

- 1 whole chicken, cut into parts
- 6 cups chicken broth
- 2 cups all-purpose flour
- 1 tablespoon baking powder
- 1/2 teaspoon salt
- 1 cup milk
- 1/2 cup unsalted butter
- 1 cup frozen peas
- Salt and pepper, to taste
- Fresh parsley, chopped (for garnish)

Instructions:

1. Put the chicken parts and chicken stock in a large pot. Bring to a boil, lower the heat and let it cook slowly until the chicken is done.
2. Make the dumplings while the chicken is cooking. Whisk the flour, baking powder, and salt together in a bowl. Add the milk and mix it until it's all mixed in.
3. Take the cooked chicken out of the pot with the chicken and cut the meat. Put the chicken shreds back into the pot.
4. Melt the butter in a different pot. Spread out spoonfuls of the dumpling batter in the already simmering soup. Put a lid on top and cook for 15 minutes or until they are fully cooked.
5. Put the frozen peas in the pot and cook for five more minutes.
6. Add pepper and salt to taste. Before serving, sprinkle with chopped fresh parsley.

BAKED ZITI BLISS:

Ingredients:

- 1 pound ziti pasta
- 2 tablespoons olive oil
- 1 onion, chopped
- 2 cloves garlic, minced
- 1 pound ground beef or Italian sausage
- 1 can (28 ounces) crushed tomatoes
- 1 teaspoon dried oregano
- 1 teaspoon dried basil
- Salt and pepper, to taste
- 2 cups ricotta cheese

- 2 cups shredded mozzarella cheese
- 1/2 cup grated Parmesan cheese
- Fresh basil, chopped (for garnish)

Instructions:

1. Follow the directions on the package to cook the ziti pasta. Remove the water and set it aside.
2. Put the olive oil in a big pan and heat it over medium-low heat. Please put in the chopped onion and cook it until it gets soft.
3. Add the minced garlic and cook for another one to two minutes, until the garlic smells good.
4. Put the Italian sausage or ground beef in the pan and cook it until it turns brown. Get rid of extra fat.
5. Add the pesto, basil, oregano, salt, and pepper, and mix them in. Let it cook for 15 to 20 minutes.
6. Warm the oven up to 190°C (375°F).
7. The cooked ziti, ricotta cheese, and half of the mozzarella and Parmesan cheese should all be put together in a big bowl.
8. Put half the pasta mixture and half the meat sauce in a baking dish. Do the stages again.
9. Add the rest of the mozzarella and Parmesan cheese on top.
10. Please put it in an already hot oven and bake for 25 to 30 minutes or until the cheese melts and bubbles.
11. Before serving, top with chopped fresh basil.

SHEPHERD'S PIE SERENITY:

Ingredients:

- 1 pound ground lamb or beef
- 1 onion, chopped
- 2 carrots, diced
- 2 cloves garlic, minced
- 2 tablespoons all-purpose flour
- 1 cup beef or vegetable broth
- 1 tablespoon tomato paste
- 1 teaspoon Worcestershire sauce
- 1 cup frozen peas
- Salt and pepper, to taste
- 4 cups mashed potatoes
- Fresh parsley, chopped (for garnish)

Instructions:

1. Warm the oven up to 200°C/400°F.
2. Warm the ground lamb or beef in a big pan over medium-low heat until it turns brown. Get rid of extra fat.
3. To the pan, add the chopped onion, carrots, and garlic. Make sure the veggies are soft.
4. Add the flour to the meat and veggies and mix them.
5. Add the Worcestershire sauce, tomato paste, and stock. Mix it around until it gets thicker.
6. Season with salt and pepper to taste, then add the frozen peas. For an extra 5 minutes, cook.
7. Move the mix of meat and vegetables to a baking dish.
8. Making an even layer, spread the mashed potatoes over the top.
9. Please put it in a hot oven and bake it for 20 to 25 minutes or until the top is golden brown.
10. Before serving, sprinkle with chopped fresh parsley.

BUTTERMILK FRIED CHICKEN COMFORT:

Ingredients:

- 2 lbs chicken pieces (drumsticks, thighs, wings)
- 2 cups buttermilk
- 2 cups all-purpose flour
- 1 tablespoon paprika
- 1 tablespoon garlic powder
- 1 tablespoon onion powder
- Salt and pepper to taste
- Vegetable oil for frying

Instructions:

1. Put the chicken pieces in buttermilk and let them sit for at least two hours or overnight in the fridge.
2. Put flour, paprika, garlic powder, onion powder, salt, and pepper in a small dish.
3. In a big pan or deep fryer, heat the vegetable oil to 350°F (175°C).
4. Be sure to coat all chicken pieces equally with the seasoned flour mix.
5. Step by step, fry the chicken until it turns golden brown and is fully cooked. Based on the pieces ' size, this should take between 15 and 20 minutes.
6. Put the clothes to dry and serve the food hot.

POT ROAST PERFECTION:

Ingredients:

- 3-4 lbs chuck roast
- 2 tablespoons vegetable oil
- 1 onion, chopped
- 3 carrots, peeled and sliced

- 3 potatoes, peeled and diced
- 4 cloves garlic, minced
- 2 cups beef broth
- 1 cup red wine (optional)
- 2 tablespoons tomato paste
- 1 teaspoon dried thyme
- Salt and pepper to taste

Instructions:

1. Add salt and pepper to the chuck roast.
2. Put vegetable oil in a big pot or Dutch oven and heat it over medium-high heat. Make sure all sides of the roast are cooked.
3. Peel and cut the carrots and potatoes into chunks. Mince the garlic and add it to the pot.
4. Red wine, tomato paste, beef broth, and dried thyme should all be mixed. Could you put it on top of the roast and veggies?
5. Bring to a simmer, then cover and put in an oven that is already hot to 325°F (160°C). After 2.5 to 3 hours, the meat should be soft enough to cut with a fork.
6. Present the pot roast with the sides and the cooking water.

LASAGNA LOVE:

Ingredients:

- 1 lb ground beef
- 1 onion, chopped
- 3 cloves garlic, minced
- 1 can (28 oz) crushed tomatoes

- 2 cans (6 oz each) tomato paste
- 2 teaspoons dried basil
- 2 teaspoons dried oregano
- Salt and pepper to taste
- 9 lasagna noodles, cooked and drained
- 3 cups ricotta cheese
- 3 cups shredded mozzarella cheese
- 1 cup grated Parmesan cheese
- Fresh basil for garnish

Instructions:

1. Toast the ground beef in a big pan over medium-low heat. Put in the crushed garlic and chopped onion and cook until the onions are soft.
2. Add tomato sauce, dried basil and oregano, salt, and pepper, and mix them in. Let it cook for 20 to 30 minutes.
3. Warm the oven up to 190°C (375°F).
4. Put lasagna noodles, meat sauce, ricotta cheese, mozzarella cheese, and Parmesan cheese in a baking dish in that order. Keep going until all the ingredients are used up. Add a layer of cheese on top to finish.
5. After the oven is hot, bake for 30 to 40 minutes or until hot and bubbly.
6. Before serving, sprinkle with fresh basil.

GRILLED CHEESE AND TOMATO SOUP HARMONY:

Ingredients for Grilled Cheese:

- Bread slices
- Butter

- Cheese slices (cheddar, Swiss, or your choice)

Ingredients for Tomato Soup:

- 2 tablespoons olive oil
- 1 onion, chopped
- 2 cloves garlic, minced
- 2 cans (28 oz each) of crushed tomatoes
- 4 cups vegetable or chicken broth
- 1 teaspoon dried basil
- Salt and pepper to taste
- 1/2 cup heavy cream (optional)

Instructions for Grilled Cheese:

1. There should be butter on one side of every piece of bread.
2. Spread butter on one side of two slices of bread and put a slice of cheese between them.
3. The sandwiches should be grilled in a pan over medium-low heat until the cheese melts and the bread turns golden brown.
4. How to Make Tomato Soup:
5.
6. Bring olive oil to a medium-low temperature in a big pot. Add the crushed garlic and chopped onion and cook until the onion is soft.
7. Salt and pepper to taste. Add crushed tomatoes, chicken or veggie broth, dried basil, and more. Bring to a low boil, then cook for 15 to 20 minutes.

8. Heavy cream can be added to make the soup creamier if you want to.
9. Make the soup smooth by blending it with an electric blender. You could also move it to a blender in batches.
10. Eating the grilled cheese sandwiches with a bowl of tomato soup will be nice.

SOUTHERN BISCUITS AND GRAVY:

Ingredients:

- 1 pound breakfast sausage
- 1/4 cup all-purpose flour
- 3 cups milk
- Salt and black pepper to taste
- Biscuits (store-bought or homemade)

Instructions:

1. The morning sausage should be cooked in a pan over medium-low heat until it turns brown.
2. Put some flour on top of the sausage and mix it in. Cook for a minute or two.
3. Add the milk slowly while stirring all the time to avoid lumps. Keep cooking until the mixture gets thicker.
4. To taste, add salt and black pepper.
5. You can put the sausage gravy on top of warm bread.

CORNBREAD CHILI CASSEROLE:

Ingredients:

- 1 pound ground beef
- 1 onion, diced
- 1 bell pepper, diced
- 2 cloves garlic, minced

- 1 can (15 oz) chili beans
- 1 can (15 oz) corn, drained
- 1 can (15 oz) diced tomatoes
- 1 package cornbread mix

Instructions:

1. Follow the directions on the cornbread mix to heat the oven.
2. Make the ground beef brown in a pan with garlic, onion, and bell pepper.
3. After getting rid of the extra fat, add corn, chilli beans, and diced tomatoes. Let it cook for 5 to 10 minutes.
4. Put the chilli mix into a baking dish.
5. Follow the directions on the cornbread mix box to make it, then spread it on top of the chilli.
6. Warm the oven up and put the cornbread until it turns golden brown.

CHICKEN AND RICE CASSEROLE CLASSIC:

Ingredients:

- 2 cups cooked chicken, shredded
- 2 cups cooked rice
- 1 can (10.5 oz) cream of mushroom soup
- 1 cup chicken broth
- 1 cup frozen peas and carrots
- 1 cup shredded cheddar cheese
- Salt and pepper to taste

Instructions:

1. Warm the oven up to 175°F (350°F).

2. Chicken shreds, cooked rice, cream of mushroom soup, chicken broth, peas, and carrots should all be put in a big bowl.
3. Add pepper and salt to taste, and then mix everything well.
4. Put the mixture in a baking dish that has been greased, and then sprinkle shredded cheddar cheese on top.
5. It should be baked for 25 to 30 minutes or until the cheese melts and bubbles.

CLASSIC CLAM CHOWDER:

Ingredients:

- 4 slices bacon, chopped
- 1 onion, finely diced
- 2 celery stalks, diced
- 3 cups potatoes, peeled and diced
- 2 cans (6.5 oz each) of minced clams with juice
- 2 cups chicken broth
- 2 cups whole milk
- 1/4 cup all-purpose flour
- Salt and pepper to taste

Instructions:

1. Cook the bacon until it's crispy in a big pot.
2. Put chopped onion and celery in the pot and cook them until they get soft.
3. To make a roux, stir in flour.
4. Add the chicken broth slowly while stirring to avoid lumps.
5. Put in milk, chopped potatoes, and clam juice. Keep cooking until the potatoes are soft.
6. Add the chopped clams and season with salt and pepper.

7. Let it cook for another 10 to 15 minutes before serving.

BEEF AND BROCCOLI:

Ingredients:

- 1 lb flank steak, thinly sliced
- 1 lb broccoli, cut into florets
- 1/2 cup low-sodium soy sauce
- 1/4 cup oyster sauce
- 2 tablespoons hoisin sauce
- 2 tablespoons brown sugar
- 3 cloves garlic, minced
- 1 tablespoon ginger, minced
- 2 tablespoons vegetable oil
- 1 tablespoon cornstarch (optional for thickening)
- Sesame seeds and green onions for garnish
- Cooked rice for serving

Instructions:

1. Soy sauce, oyster sauce, hoisin sauce, and brown sugar should all be mixed in a bowl. Put away.
2. Heat vegetable oil in a big pan or wok over medium-high heat.
3. Stir-fry the flank steak slices until they turn brown. Take the meat out of the pan and set it aside.
4. If you need to, add more oil to the same pan and stir-fry the garlic and ginger until they smell good.
5. Stir-fry the broccoli pieces until they are soft but still have some crunch.
6. Put the cooked beef back in the pan and add the broccoli. Then, pour the sauce over the meat and broccoli. Mix things well.

7. Make a mixture with cornstarch and a tablespoon of water if you want the sauce to be thicker. Stir it into the sauce in the pan until it gets thicker.
8. Put chopped green onions and sesame seeds on top.
9. Could you put it on top of cooked rice?

HOMESTYLE CHICKEN AND NOODLES:

Ingredients:

- 1 lb boneless, skinless chicken breasts cut into bite-sized pieces
- 8 oz egg noodles
- 2 tablespoons olive oil
- 1 onion, finely chopped
- 2 carrots, sliced
- 2 celery stalks, sliced
- 3 cloves garlic, minced
- 4 cups chicken broth
- 1 teaspoon dried thyme
- Salt and pepper to taste
- Fresh parsley for garnish (optional)

Instructions:

1. Follow the directions on the package to cook the egg noodles. Remove the water and set it aside.
2. Put olive oil in a big pot and heat it over medium-low heat. Chop up the celery, carrots, and onion and add them. Cook the veggies until they get soft.
3. Add the minced garlic and cook for one more minute.
4. Please put in the chicken pieces and cook them until all sides are cooked.
5. Add the chicken broth and thyme leaves that have been dried. Add pepper and salt to taste.

6. Once it starts to boil, lower the heat and let it cook slowly until the chicken is fully cooked.
7. Put the cooked egg noodles in the pot and mix them in.
8. Add fresh parsley as a garnish if you like.
9. Warm up and serve.

HEALTHY AND LIGHT FARE:

QUINOA AND KALE SALAD BOWL:

Ingredients:

- 1 cup quinoa, rinsed
- 2 cups water or vegetable broth
- 1 bunch kale, stems removed and leaves chopped
- 1 cup cherry tomatoes, halved
- 1 cucumber, diced
- 1/2 red onion, finely chopped
- 1/4 cup feta cheese, crumbled
- 1/4 cup extra virgin olive oil
- 2 tablespoons balsamic vinegar
- Salt and pepper to taste

Instructions:

1. Follow the directions on the package to cook the quinoa with water or veggie broth.
2. Put cooked quinoa, kale, cherry tomatoes, cucumber, red onion, and feta cheese in a big bowl.
3. Salt and pepper should be mixed with olive oil in a small bowl.
4. Add the sauce to the salad and mix it all.
5. Serve cold.

GRILLED SALMON WITH LEMON DILL SAUCE:

Ingredients:

- 4 salmon fillets
- Salt and black pepper to taste
- 2 tablespoons olive oil
- 2 tablespoons fresh lemon juice
- 1 tablespoon fresh dill, chopped

Instructions:

1. Warm up the grill over medium-high heat.
2. Add salt and black pepper to the salmon pieces.
3. Put the steaks on the grill and brush them with olive oil.
4. The fish should be cooked on each grill side for four to five minutes.
5. Put chopped dill and lemon juice in a small bowl and mix them.
6. Before serving, pour the lemon-dill sauce over the grilled salmon.

ZUCCHINI NOODLE PESTO PRIMAVERA:

Ingredients:

- 4 medium-sized zucchini, spiralized into noodles
- 1 cup cherry tomatoes, halved
- 1 bell pepper, thinly sliced
- 1/2 cup black olives, sliced
- 1/4 cup pine nuts
- 1/2 cup pesto sauce
- Salt and black pepper to taste
- Grated Parmesan cheese (optional)

Instructions:

1. Cook zucchini noodles, cherry tomatoes, bell pepper, and black olives in a large pan until the veggies are soft.
2. When you add the pine nuts and pesto sauce to the pan, toss the noodles and veggies to cover them all.
3. To taste, add salt and black pepper.
4. No need to: Grate some Parmesan cheese on top before serving.

MEDITERRANEAN CHICKPEA SALAD:

Ingredients:

- 2 cans (15 oz each) chickpeas, drained and rinsed
- 1 cucumber, diced
- 1 cup cherry tomatoes, halved
- 1/2 red onion, finely chopped
- 1/2 cup Kalamata olives, sliced
- 1/2 cup feta cheese, crumbled
- 1/4 cup fresh parsley, chopped
- 1/4 cup extra virgin olive oil
- 2 tablespoons red wine vinegar
- 1 teaspoon dried oregano
- Salt and black pepper to taste

Instructions:

1. Add the cucumber, cherry tomatoes, red onion, olives, feta cheese, and parsley to a big bowl.
2. Mix olive oil, red wine vinegar, salt, black pepper, and dried oregano in a small bowl with a whisk.
3. Add the sauce to the salad and mix it all.
4. Serve cold.

SHRIMP AND AVOCADO LETTUCE WRAPS:

Ingredients:

- 1 lb shrimp, peeled and deveined
- 2 avocados, diced
- 1 cup cherry tomatoes, halved
- 1/4 cup red onion, finely chopped
- 1/4 cup cilantro, chopped
- 2 tablespoons lime juice
- Salt and pepper to taste
- Lettuce leaves for wrapping

Instructions:

1. Cook the shrimp in a pan until they are pink and opaque.
2. Put the chopped avocados, cherry tomatoes, red onion, cilantro, and lime juice in a bowl. Add the cooked shrimp.
3. Add pepper and salt to taste.
4. Put the shrimp and avocado mix on top of the leaf leaves.
5. Serve right away, and enjoy your tasty lettuce wraps!

TURKEY AND VEGETABLE SKEWER DELIGHT:

Ingredients:

- 1 lb turkey, breast, cut into cubes
- 2 bell peppers, cut into chunks
- 1 red onion, cut into chunks
- Cherry tomatoes
- 1 zucchini, sliced
- Olive oil
- 1 teaspoon dried oregano
- Salt and pepper to taste

Instructions:

1. Warm up the grill or grill pan.

2. Put bell peppers, red onion, cherry tomatoes, zucchini, and turkey cubes in a bowl.
3. Add some olive oil and salt, pepper, and dried oregano to taste.
4. Put the veggies and turkey on skewers.
5. Put the veggies and turkey on the grill until the turkey is fully cooked.
6. Do not cool the skewers down.

SWEET POTATO AND BLACK BEAN BOWL:

Ingredients:

- 2 sweet potatoes, peeled and diced
- 1 can black beans, drained and rinsed
- 1 cup corn kernels
- 1 red bell pepper, diced
- 1 avocado, sliced
- 1/4 cup cilantro, chopped
- Lime wedges
- Salt and pepper to taste

Instructions:

1. Either steam or roast the sweet potatoes until they are soft.
2. Put black beans, corn, red bell pepper, parsley, and sweet potatoes in a bowl.
3. Add pepper and salt to taste.
4. Cut up some avocado and put it on top. Serve with lime wedges.

LEMON GARLIC SHRIMP QUINOA:

Ingredients:

- 1 lb shrimp, peeled and deveined
- 1 cup quinoa, rinsed
- 2 cups chicken or vegetable broth
- 3 cloves garlic, minced
- Zest and juice of 1 lemon
- 2 tablespoons olive oil
- Salt and pepper to taste
- Fresh parsley for garnish

Instructions:

1. Follow the directions on the package to cook the quinoa with chicken or veggie broth.
2. Put olive oil in a pan and heat it over medium-low heat.
3. Mix in the garlic and cook until it smells good.
4. Put shrimp in the pan and cook them until they are pink and opaque.
5. Add the lemon juice and zest, and mix well.
6. Add pepper and salt to taste.
7. Put the shrimp with lemon and garlic on top of the rice.
8. Add fresh parsley as a garnish.

GREEK YOGURT CHICKEN SALAD:

Ingredients:

- 2 cups cooked chicken breast, shredded
- 1 cup Greek yogurt
- 1 cucumber, diced
- 1 cup cherry tomatoes, halved
- 1/2 red onion, finely chopped
- 1/4 cup feta cheese, crumbled
- 2 tablespoons fresh dill, chopped
- Salt and pepper to taste

Instructions:

1. Shred the chicken and mix it with Greek yoghurt, cucumber, cherry tomatoes, red onion, and feta cheese in a big bowl.
2. Good mix everything until the Greek yoghurt covers everything evenly.
3. To taste, add chopped dill, salt, and pepper. Mix it again.
4. Please put it in the fridge for at least 30 minutes before serving so the tastes can mix.
5. Enjoy! Serve cold.

CAULIFLOWER RICE STIR-FRY:

Ingredients:

- 1 medium-sized cauliflower, riced
- 1 cup broccoli florets
- 1 bell pepper, thinly sliced
- 1 carrot, julienned
- 1 cup snap peas, trimmed
- 2 tablespoons soy sauce
- 1 tablespoon sesame oil
- 1 tablespoon olive oil
- 2 cloves garlic, minced
- 1 teaspoon ginger, grated
- Green onions, chopped (for garnish)

Instructions:

1. Heat the olive oil over medium-low heat in a big pan or wok.
2. Grate the ginger and chop the garlic. Sauté for one to two minutes until the food smells good.

3. Put broccoli, bell pepper, carrot, snap peas, and riced cauliflower into the pan.
4. The veggies should be stir-fried until they are soft but still have some crunch.
5. Put soy sauce and sesame oil in a small bowl and mix them. Add the sauce to the stir-fry and mix it all.
6. Add two to three more minutes of cooking.
7. Add some chopped green onions on top and serve.

CAPRESE STUFFED PORTOBELLO MUSHROOMS:

Ingredients:

- 4 large Portobello mushrooms, stems removed
- 1 cup cherry tomatoes, halved
- 1 cup fresh mozzarella, diced
- 1/4 cup fresh basil, chopped
- 2 tablespoons balsamic glaze
- Salt and pepper to taste
- Olive oil for brushing

Instructions:

1. Warm the oven up to 190°C (375°F).
2. Put the Portobello mushrooms on a baking sheet and use olive oil to cover both sides.
3. Mix chopped basil, cherry tomatoes, and fresh mozzarella in a bowl.
4. Take the tomato and cheese mixture and put some inside each Portobello mushroom.
5. Add pepper and salt to taste.
6. Please put it in the oven and bake for 15 to 20 minutes, or until the cheese melts and the mushrooms soften.
7. Add the vinegar glaze right before serving.

TUNA AND WHITE BEAN SALAD:

Ingredients:

- 2 cans (15 oz each) white beans, drained and rinsed
- 2 cans (5 oz each) tuna, drained
- 1 red onion, finely chopped
- 1/4 cup fresh parsley, chopped
- 1/4 cup olive oil
- 2 tablespoons red wine vinegar
- Salt and pepper to taste
- Lemon wedges for serving

Instructions:

1. Put white beans, tuna, red onion, and fresh parsley in a big bowl.
2. Mix olive oil and red wine vinegar in a small bowl with a whisk.
3. Add the sauce to the bean and tuna mix and gently toss to mix.
4. Add pepper and salt to taste.
5. Please put it in the fridge for at least 30 minutes before you serve it.
6. Put lemon wedges on the side and serve.

TERIYAKI TOFU BUDDHA BOWL:

Ingredients:

- 1 cup extra-firm tofu, cubed
- 2 tablespoons soy sauce
- 1 tablespoon teriyaki sauce
- 1 tablespoon sesame oil
- 1 cup broccoli florets
- 1 cup carrots, julienned

- 1 cup red cabbage, shredded
- 1 cup cooked brown rice or quinoa
- Sesame seeds for garnish
- Green onions, sliced, for garnish

Instructions:

1. First, press the tofu to get rid of the extra water. Then, cut it into cubes.
2. Mix the soy sauce, teriyaki sauce, and sesame oil in a bowl. Put the tofu in this mixture and let it sit for at least 30 minutes.
3. Warm the oven up to 200°C/400°F.
4. Put broccoli, carrots, and tofu marinating on a baking sheet for twenty to twenty-five minutes or until the veggies are soft and the tofu is golden.
5. Put cooked rice or quinoa, roasted tofu, and veggies in the bowl.
6. Put green onions and sesame seeds on top to make it look nice.

ROASTED VEGETABLE QUINOA BOWL:

Ingredients:

- 1 cup quinoa, rinsed
- 2 cups mixed vegetables (zucchini, bell peppers, cherry tomatoes, etc.), chopped
- 2 tablespoons olive oil
- 1 teaspoon dried thyme
- Salt and pepper to taste
- 1/4 cup feta cheese, crumbled (optional)
- Fresh basil for garnish

Instructions:

1. Warm the oven up to 200°C/400°F.
2. Add olive oil, thyme, salt, and pepper to the chopped veggies and toss them around.
3. Spread the veggies out on a baking sheet. Roast them for twenty to twenty-five minutes or until soft and golden.
4. Follow the directions on the package to cook the quinoa while the veggies are roasting.
5. Put the cooked quinoa and roasted veggies in the bowl.
6. If you want, you can sprinkle chopped feta cheese on top and fresh basil on top.

SPINACH AND STRAWBERRY SALAD:

Ingredients:

- 4 cups fresh spinach leaves, washed and dried
- 1 cup strawberries, hulled and sliced
- 1/4 cup feta cheese, crumbled
- 1/4 cup sliced almonds
- Balsamic vinaigrette dressing

Instructions:

1. Put the spinach, feta cheese, sliced almonds, and strawberries in a big bowl.
2. Add the balsamic vinaigrette sauce and gently toss everything together.
3. Serve right away.

CHICKPEA AND CUCUMBER GREEK SALAD:

Ingredients:

- 1 can (15 oz) chickpeas, drained and rinsed
- 1 cucumber, diced
- 1 cup cherry tomatoes, halved

- 1/2 red onion, finely chopped
- 1/2 cup Kalamata olives, sliced
- 1/2 cup feta cheese, crumbled
- 3 tablespoons olive oil
- 2 tablespoons red wine vinegar
- 1 teaspoon dried oregano
- Salt and pepper to taste

Instructions:

1. Put chickpeas, cucumber, cherry tomatoes, red onion, olives, and feta cheese in a big bowl.
2. Mix olive oil, red wine vinegar, dried oregano, salt, and pepper in a small bowl with a whisk.
3. Give the salad a gentle toss to coat it with the sauce.
4. Please put it in the fridge for at least 30 minutes before serving so the tastes can mix.

SALMON AND ASPARAGUS FOIL PACKETS:

Ingredients:

- 4 salmon fillets
- 1 bunch of asparagus, trimmed
- 2 tablespoons olive oil
- 2 cloves garlic, minced
- 1 lemon, sliced
- Salt and pepper to taste
- Fresh dill for garnish (optional)

Instructions:

1. Warm the oven up to 200°C (400°F).

2. Make four pieces of foil big enough to fit a salmon fillet and some asparagus on each one.
3. Put a piece of salmon in the middle of each piece of foil.
4. Spread the asparagus out around the salmon piece.
5. Add a little olive oil to each salmon fillet and asparagus.
6. Spread the minced garlic out evenly on top of the asparagus and fillets.
7. Put a few pieces of lemon on top of each salmon fillet.
8. Add pepper and salt to taste.
9. To make a packet, fold the sides of the foil over the salmon and asparagus. Make sure the edges are well sealed.
10. The foil packets should be put on a baking sheet. The salmon should be cooked through and flaky with a fork after about 15 to 20 minutes in a preheated oven.
11. Carefully open the foil packets; if you want, sprinkle with fresh dill. Then serve.

PESTO ZOODLE SALAD SUPREME:

Ingredients:

- 4 medium zucchini, spiralized into noodles
- 1 cup cherry tomatoes, halved
- 1/2 cup black olives, sliced
- 1/4 cup pine nuts, toasted
- 1/2 cup feta cheese, crumbled
- 1/2 cup fresh basil leaves, chopped
- 1/3 cup pesto sauce
- Salt and pepper to taste

Instructions:

1. Put the zucchini noodles, cherry tomatoes, black olives, pine nuts, feta cheese, and fresh basil in a big bowl to make the dish.
2. Mix the pesto sauce into the bowl and toss the food until everything is well-covered.
3. Add pepper and salt to taste.
4. Put the salad in the fridge for about 30 minutes before serving it so the tastes can mix.
5. As a cool side meal, serve the Pesto Zoodle Salad Supreme.

SWEET ENDINGS:

DECADENT CHOCOLATE AVOCADO MOUSSE:

Ingredients:

- 2 ripe avocados
- 1/2 cup cocoa powder
- 1/2 cup maple syrup or honey
- 1/3 cup almond milk
- 1 teaspoon vanilla extract
- Pinch of salt

Instructions:

1. Take the avocado meat out and put it in a blender or food processor.
2. A pinch of salt, maple syrup (or honey), almond milk, and cocoa powder should all be added.
3. To make it smooth and creamy, scrape down the sides of the bowl as needed.
4. Put the mousse into bowls or glasses to serve.
5. Please put it in the fridge for at least 30 minutes before you serve it.

6. Add fresh berries or a dollop of whipped cream as a treat if you want to.

BERRY BLISS CHEESECAKE BITES:

Ingredients:

- 1 cup graham cracker crumbs
- 1/4 cup melted butter
- 16 oz cream cheese, softened
- 1/2 cup sugar
- 1 teaspoon vanilla extract
- Assorted berries for topping

Instructions:

1. Put graham cracker pieces and melted butter in a bowl and mix them. To make the crust, press the batter into the bottom of a mini muffin tin that has been lined.
2. Cream cheese, sugar, and vanilla extract should be mixed in a different bowl until smooth.
3. Put the cream cheese mixture on top of the muffin tin's crust.
4. Please put it in the fridge for at least two hours or until it sets.
5. Before serving, put a different kind of berry on top of each cheesecake bite.

APPLE CINNAMON CRISP COMFORT:

Ingredients:

- 4 cups sliced apples (peeled and cored)
- 1 tablespoon lemon juice
- 1/2 cup rolled oats
- 1/4 cup flour

- 1/4 cup brown sugar
- 1/2 teaspoon ground cinnamon
- 1/4 cup melted butter

Instructions:

1. Warm the oven up to 175°F (350°F).
2. Spread sliced apples in a baking dish after mixing them with lemon juice.
3. Mix oats, flour, brown sugar, and cinnamon in a bowl.
4. Pour the melted butter over the oat mix and mix it in until it is crumbly.
5. Spread the oat mixture out over the apples in a thin layer.
6. It should be baked for 30 to 35 minutes or until the top is golden brown and the apples are soft.
7. If you want, you can serve it warm with a scoop of vanilla ice cream.

LEMON BLUEBERRY PARFAIT PERFECTION:

Ingredients:

- 1 cup Greek yogurt
- 2 tablespoons honey
- Zest of 1 lemon
- 1 cup fresh blueberries
- Granola for layering

Instructions:

1. Add honey and lemon juice to a bowl and mix the Greek yoghurt with them.
2. Put yoghurt, fresh blueberries, and granola in serving glasses, one on top of the other.
3. Add more layers until the glass is full, and top it off with a dollop of yoghurt.

4. You can add more blueberries and a drop of honey as a decoration if you want to.
5. Please put it in the fridge for at least 30 minutes before you serve it.

CHOCOLATE PEANUT BUTTER BANANA BREAD:

Ingredients:

- 3 ripe bananas, mashed
- 1/2 cup peanut butter
- 1/4 cup melted butter
- 1 teaspoon vanilla extract
- 1 egg
- 1 teaspoon baking soda
- Pinch of salt
- 1/2 cup sugar
- 1 1/2 cups all-purpose flour
- 1/4 cup cocoa powder
- 1/2 cup chocolate chips (optional)

Instructions:

1. Warm the oven up to 175°F (350°F). Prepare a bread pan by greasing it.
2. Mash the bananas in a big bowl. It's time to add the egg, peanut butter, melted butter, and vanilla extract. Combine well.
3. Mix in the cocoa powder, salt, baking soda, and flour. Don't mix any further than that.
4. You can add chocolate chips if you want to.
5. Put the batter into the loaf pan that has been made. Bake for about an hour to seventy minutes or until a toothpick stuck in the middle comes out clean.

6. Let the banana bread cool down before cutting it into pieces.

MANGO COCONUT RICE PUDDING:

Ingredients:

- 1 cup jasmine rice
- 2 cups coconut milk
- 1 cup mango puree
- 1/2 cup sugar
- 1/2 teaspoon vanilla extract
- Pinch of salt
- Mango slices and shredded coconut for garnish (optional)

Instructions:

1. Run cold water over the rice until the water is clear.
2. Put rice, coconut milk, mango puree, sugar, vanilla extract, and salt in a pot.
3. Once it starts to boil, lower the heat, cover, and let it cook for 20 to 25 minutes, or until the rice is done and the sauce has thickened.
4. To keep things from sticking, stir every so often.
5. Let it cool down a bit after it's done cooking before serving. You can add mango pieces and shredded coconut as a garnish if you want.

RASPBERRY ALMOND TART DELIGHT:

Ingredients:

- 1 pre-made pie crust
- 1 cup almond meal
- 1/4 cup sugar
- 1/4 cup melted butter

- 1 cup fresh raspberries
- 1/4 cup raspberry jam

Instructions:

1. Follow the directions on the pie crust to get your oven ready.
2. Melt the butter and add the almond meal to a bowl.
3. Put the nut mixture into the pie crust that has already been made.
4. The crust should be baked for the time given in the directions or until it turns golden brown.
5. Spread raspberry jam over the bottom of the bread once it is cool.
6. Fresh strawberries should be put on top.
7. Please put it in the fridge to cool down before serving.

DARK CHOCOLATE RASPBERRY FONDUE:

Ingredients:

- 1 cup dark chocolate, chopped
- 1/2 cup heavy cream
- 1 teaspoon vanilla extract
- Fresh raspberries and other dippable (strawberries, marshmallows, pretzels)

Instructions:

1. Put the heavy cream in a pot and heat it until it just starts to simmer.
2. Take it off the heat and add the chopped dark chocolate. After one minute, stir it until it's smooth.
3. Add vanilla flavour and stir.
4. Move the chocolate mix to a bowl that can handle heat or a fondue pot.

5. Serve with fresh strawberries and other things that you can dip.

PUMPKIN SPICE CUPCAKE ELEGANCE:

Ingredients:

- 1 3/4 cups all-purpose flour
- 1 teaspoon baking powder
- 1/2 teaspoon baking soda
- 1/2 teaspoon salt
- 1 teaspoon ground cinnamon
- 1/2 teaspoon ground ginger
- 1/4 teaspoon ground nutmeg
- 1/4 teaspoon ground cloves
- 1/2 cup unsalted butter, softened
- 1 cup granulated sugar
- 2 large eggs
- 1 cup canned pumpkin puree
- 1/2 cup buttermilk
- 1 teaspoon vanilla extract

Instructions:

1. Warm your oven to 350°F (175°C) and put paper cups in a cupcake pan.
2. Mix the flour, baking powder, baking soda, salt, and spices in a medium-sized bowl using a whisk.
3. Mix the softened butter and sugar in a big bowl until the mixture is light and fluffy.
4. Add the eggs and beat well after each one, one at a time. Add the pumpkin juice and mix it in.
5. Slowly add the dry ingredients to the wet ones, mixing in the buttermilk occasionally. Put the dry ingredients in

first and end with them. Add the vanilla extract and mix well.

6. Fill up each cupcake tin two-thirds of the way to the top with batter.
7. Please put it in the oven and bake for 18 to 20 minutes or until a toothpick stuck in the middle comes out clean.
8. Let the cupcakes cool down before you frost them.

SALTED CARAMEL CHOCOLATE TORTE:

Ingredients:

- 1 1/2 cups chocolate cookie crumbs
- 1/2 cup unsalted butter, melted
- 1 cup semi-sweet chocolate chips
- 1 cup heavy cream
- 1 cup caramel sauce (store-bought or homemade)
- 1 teaspoon sea salt flakes

Instructions:

1. Warm the oven up to 175°F (350°F).
2. Put the chocolate cookie crumbs and melted butter in a bowl and mix them. Press the batter into the bottom of a springform pan to make the crust.
3. Put the heavy cream in a pot and heat it until it boils. Pour it over the chocolate chips in a bowl that can handle heat. After one minute, stir it until it's smooth.
4. Spread the chocolate frosting on top of the pan's crust.
5. Put the pan in the fridge for at least two hours to set.
6. Put some caramel sauce on top of the chocolate after it's set.
7. On top of the caramel, sprinkle sea salt flakes.
8. Please put it back in the fridge for two more hours before serving.

KEY LIME PIE PARFAIT:

Ingredients:

- 1 1/2 cups graham cracker crumbs
- 1/2 cup unsalted butter, melted
- 1 cup key lime juice
- 1 tablespoon key lime zest
- 1 can (14 ounces) sweetened condensed milk
- 2 cups heavy cream
- 1/4 cup powdered sugar
- Additional lime slices for garnish

Instructions:

1. Mix the graham cracker crumbs and hot butter in a bowl. Press the mixture into the bottom of the serving cups to make the crust.
2. Whisk the key lime juice, zest, and sweetened condensed milk in a different bowl until everything is well mixed.
3. Put some graham cracker crust in each glass and pour the key lime blend.
4. Mix the powdered sugar and heavy cream in a different bowl and whip them together until stiff peaks form.
5. Put some key lime on the bottom and then some whipped cream in each glass.
6. Add more lime slices as a garnish.
7. Please put it in the fridge for at least two hours before you serve it.

PISTACHIO AND CRANBERRY ENERGY BITES:

Ingredients:

- 1 cup old-fashioned oats
- 1/2 cup pistachios, chopped

- 1/2 cup dried cranberries, chopped
- 1/3 cup honey
- 1/2 cup almond butter
- 1 teaspoon vanilla extract
- A pinch of salt

Instructions:

1. Mix the oats, chopped pistachios, and dried cranberries in a big bowl.
2. Low heat should be used to melt the honey and almond butter in a small pot. Take it off the heat and add the vanilla extract and a little salt.
3. Add the honey-almond butter mix to the dry ingredients and mix them well to cover everything.
4. Put the mixture in the fridge for about 30 minutes to make it easier to work with.
5. Once the mixture is cold, roll it into balls that are easy to eat.
6. Put the energy bites on a baking sheet lined with parchment paper and chill them for another 30 minutes.
7. Keep the energy bites in a jar that won't let air in the fridge.

BLACK FOREST CHERRY CHOCOLATE CAKE:

Ingredients:

- 2 cups all-purpose flour
- 1 3/4 cups granulated sugar
- 3/4 cup unsweetened cocoa powder
- 2 teaspoons baking powder
- 1 1/2 teaspoons baking soda
- 1 teaspoon salt
- 2 large eggs

- 1 cup whole milk
- 1/2 cup vegetable oil
- 2 teaspoons vanilla extract
- 1 cup boiling water
- 1 can (21 ounces) cherry pie filling
- Whipped cream for topping
- Chocolate shavings for garnish

Instructions:

1. Warm the oven up to 175°F (350°F). Butter and flour two round cake pans that are 9 inches in diameter.
2. Mix the flour, sugar, cocoa powder, baking powder, baking soda, and salt in a large bowl with a whisk.
3. After you mix the dry ingredients, add the eggs, milk, oil, and vanilla extract. Mix everything well.
4. Add the hot water and stir until the batter is smooth. It's okay that the batter is a little thick.
5. Spread the batter out evenly in the pans that have been prepared. Bake for 30 to 35 minutes or until a knife stuck in the middle comes out clean.
6. Let the cakes cool down. Spread cherry pie filling on top of one cake layer after it has cooled. Then, put the second cake layer on top and frost the whole thing with whipped cream.
7. Add more cherry pie filling and chocolate bits as a garnish.

CHIA SEED PUDDING PARFAIT:

Ingredients:

- 1/4 cup chia seeds
- 1 cup almond milk (or any milk of your choice)
- 1 tablespoon maple syrup

- 1 teaspoon vanilla extract
- Fresh berries (strawberries, blueberries, raspberries)
- Granola

Instructions:

1. Mix the chia seeds, almond milk, maple syrup, and vanilla extract into a bowl. Mix things well.
2. Put the mixture in the fridge for at least 4 hours or overnight to let the chia seeds soak up the liquid and make a pudding-like texture.
3. When the chia pudding is done, put fresh berries and granola on top of it in serving cups.
4. Do this again and again until the glasses are full.
5. If you want, you can add more berries and a drizzle of maple syrup on top.

RED VELVET TRIFLE TEMPTATION:

Ingredients:

- 1 box red velvet cake mix (and ingredients needed to prepare it)
- 2 cups cream cheese frosting
- 1 cup whipped cream
- 1 cup raspberries
- 1 cup chocolate shavings

Instructions:

1. Follow the directions on the box to make the red velvet cake. Let it cool down, and then cut it into little cubes.
2. Spread the red velvet cake cubes, cream cheese frosting, whipped cream, raspberries, and chocolate shavings in a trifle dish or individual serving cups.

3. Put more layers on top until the dish or glasses are full. Finish with a dollop of whipped cream and some chocolate shavings.
4. Please put it in the fridge for at least an hour before you serve it.

MAPLE PECAN PIE PLEASURE:

Ingredients:

- 1 pie crust (store-bought or homemade)
- 1 1/2 cups pecan halves
- 3 large eggs
- 1 cup pure maple syrup
- 1/2 cup granulated sugar
- 1/2 cup unsalted butter, melted
- 1 teaspoon vanilla extract
- 1/4 teaspoon salt

Instructions:

1. Warm the oven up to 175°F (350°F). In a 9-inch pie dish, put the pie crust.
2. Put the nut halves in the pie crust's bottom.
3. Add the eggs, maple syrup, sugar, melted butter, vanilla extract, and salt to a bowl. Use a whisk to mix the ingredients well.
4. Spread the maple syrup mix on top of the nuts in the pie crust.
5. It's done when the middle is set in the oven after 50 to 55 minutes.
6. Let the pie cool down before cutting it. If you want, you can serve it with whipped cream on top.

ORANGE CREAMSICLE CHEESECAKE CUPS:

Ingredients:

- 1 1/2 cups graham cracker crumbs
- 1/3 cup melted butter
- 1 tablespoon sugar
- 16 ounces cream cheese, softened
- 1 cup sugar
- 1 teaspoon vanilla extract
- 1/2 cup orange juice
- 1 tablespoon orange zest
- 2 cups whipped cream
- Orange slices for garnish (optional)

Instructions:

1. Put the graham cracker crumbs, melted butter, and 1 tablespoon of sugar in a medium-sized bowl and mix them well.
2. To make the crust, press the crumb mixture into the bottom of each serving cup.
3. Cream cheese should be beaten in a big bowl until it's smooth.
4. Add sugar to the cream cheese with the orange juice and zest. Mix everything well.
5. The whipped cream should be added slowly so that the mixture stays smooth and rich.
6. Put some cheesecake mix on top of the shell in each cup.
7. Put the cheesecake in the fridge for at least 4 hours or overnight to set.
8. Add orange pieces as a garnish before serving.

TIRAMISU TOFFEE TRIFLE:

Ingredients:

- 1 package of ladyfinger cookies
- 1 cup strong brewed coffee, cooled
- 1/4 cup coffee liqueur (optional)
- 8 ounces mascarpone cheese
- 1 cup heavy cream
- 1/2 cup powdered sugar
- 1 teaspoon vanilla extract
- 1 cup toffee bits
- Cocoa powder for dusting

Instructions:

1. Put the brewed coffee and coffee liquor (if using) in a shallow dish.
2. Dipping each ladyfinger in the coffee mix, be careful not to soak them too much.
3. Put a layer of dipped ladyfingers at the base of a pudding dish or glasses for serving one person at a time.
4. Mascarpone cheese, powdered sugar, and vanilla extract should all be mixed in a bowl. Mix until it's smooth.
5. Whip the heavy cream in a different bowl until stiff peaks form.
6. Mix the mascarpone and whipped cream by folding them in slowly.
7. Put some mascarpone mixture on top of the ladyfingers in the dessert dish.
8. On top of the mascarpone layer, sprinkle a layer of toffee bits.
9. Add more layers until you reach the top of the dessert dish. Add a layer of mascarpone and some toffee bits to finish.
10. Add cocoa powder to the top.

11. Please put it in the fridge for at least two to three hours before serving so the tastes can mix.

30-MINUTE CHICKEN PICCATA:

Ingredients:

- 4 boneless, skinless chicken breasts
- Salt and pepper to taste
- 1 cup all-purpose flour for dredging
- 4 tablespoons olive oil
- 1/2 cup fresh lemon juice
- 1/2 cup chicken broth
- 1/4 cup capers, drained
- 1/4 cup fresh parsley, chopped

Instructions:

1. Add salt and pepper to the chicken breasts.
2. Coat each chicken breast in flour and then shake off any extra.
3. Warm up the olive oil in a big pan over medium-high heat.
4. Put the chicken breasts in the pan and cook them on each side for three to four minutes until they turn golden brown.
5. Take the chicken out of the pan and set it aside.
6. Put chicken stock, capers, and lemon juice in the same pan. Bring up the temperature.
7. Put the chicken back in the pan and cook for another 5 minutes.
8. Add chopped parsley as a garnish before serving.

QUICK AND EASY SHRIMP STIR-FRY:

Ingredients:

- 1 pound shrimp, peeled and deveined
- 2 cups broccoli florets
- 1 bell pepper, thinly sliced
- 1 carrot, julienned
- 2 tablespoons soy sauce
- 1 tablespoon oyster sauce
- 1 tablespoon sesame oil
- 2 cloves garlic, minced
- 1 teaspoon ginger, grated
- Cooked rice for serving

Instructions:

1. Set the sesame oil on medium-high heat in a wok or big skillet.
2. Stir-fry the shrimp for two to three minutes until they turn pink. Take it out of the wok and set it away.
3. If you need to, add more oil to the same pan and cook the garlic and ginger until they smell good.
4. Put in the carrot, bell pepper, and broccoli. Stir-fry them for 3 to 4 minutes or until the vegetables are crisp-tender.
5. Put the cooked shrimp back in the pot and add oyster and soy sauce. Use a stir to mix.
6. Add two more minutes of cooking and keep going until everything is hot.
7. Could you put it on top of cooked rice?

ONE-POT SPAGHETTI BOLOGNESE:

Ingredients:

- 1 pound ground beef
- 1 onion, finely chopped

- 2 cloves garlic, minced
- 1 can (28 ounces) crushed tomatoes
- 1 cup beef broth
- 1 teaspoon dried oregano
- 1 teaspoon dried basil
- Salt and pepper to taste
- 8 ounces spaghetti
- Grated Parmesan cheese for serving

Instructions:

1. Over medium-low heat, brown the ground beef in a big pot. Get rid of extra fat.
2. Put chopped garlic and onions in the pot and cook them until they get soft.
3. Beef broth, oregano, basil, salt, and pepper should all be stirred.
4. After cutting the spaghetti in half, add it to the pot and ensure it's covered in water.
5. Let it cook on low heat for 15 to 20 minutes or until the spaghetti is done and the sauce gets thick.
6. Grate some Parmesan cheese on top and serve hot.

SPEEDY MARGHERITA PIZZA:

Ingredients:

- 1 pre-made pizza dough
- 1/2 cup pizza sauce
- 1 1/2 cups fresh mozzarella, sliced
- Fresh basil leaves
- Olive oil for drizzling
- Salt and pepper to taste

Instructions:

1. Follow the directions on the pizza dough package to heat your oven.
2. Put some flour on a table and roll out the pizza dough.
3. Take care to leave a line around the dough so that the crust can stick out.
4. On top of the sauce, put pieces of fresh mozzarella.
5. Sprinkle with olive oil and salt and pepper.
6. Place the pizza on a baking sheet or pizza stone and bake it as directed on the dough until the crust is golden and the cheese is melted and bubbly.
7. Please remove it from the oven and add fresh basil leaves before serving.

BBQ CHICKEN QUESADILLA DASH:

Ingredients:

- 2 cups cooked and shredded chicken
- 1 cup BBQ sauce
- 1 cup shredded cheddar cheese
- 1 cup shredded Monterey Jack cheese
- 1/2 cup diced red onion
- 1/4 cup chopped fresh cilantro
- 4 large flour tortillas

Instructions:

1. Put the chopped chicken in a bowl and coat it with BBQ sauce.
2. Lay out a tortilla on a flat surface. Put some of the BBQ chicken mixture on half of the bread.
3. Add some cheddar and Monterey Jack cheese to the chicken.
4. On top of the cheese, put some diced red onion and parsley.

5. To make a half-moon form, fold the tortilla in half.
6. Do this again with the rest of the tortillas.
7. On medium heat, warm up a big pan. It should be cooked on each side for two to three minutes or until the tortilla is crispy and the cheese melts.
8. Please put it on a plate and dip it in your favourite sauce.

TERIYAKI SALMON BOWLS IN A FLASH:

Ingredients:

- 4 salmon fillets
- 1/2 cup teriyaki sauce
- 2 cups cooked rice
- 1 cup broccoli florets, steamed
- 1 cup sliced carrots, steamed
- Sesame seeds and green onions for garnish

Instructions:

1. Warm the oven up to 200°C/400°F.
2. Put the salmon pieces on a baking sheet with parchment paper.
3. Put teriyaki sauce on each fish and coat it.
4. Place the fish in the oven and bake for 15 to 20 minutes or until it is fully cooked.
5. Prepare the rice, peas, and carrots while the salmon is baking.
6. Put together bowls with rice as the base and salmon, steamed broccoli, and carrots on top.
7. If you want, add more teriyaki sauce on top.
8. Put green onions and sesame seeds on top to make it look nice.

INSTANT POT CHILI CON CARNE:

Ingredients:

- 1 lb ground beef
- 1 onion, diced
- 2 cloves garlic, minced
- 1 can (15 oz) kidney beans, drained and rinsed
- 1 can (15 oz) black beans, drained and rinsed
- 1 can (15 oz) diced tomatoes
- 1 can (6 oz) tomato paste
- 1 cup beef broth
- 2 tablespoons chili powder
- 1 teaspoon cumin
- 1 teaspoon oregano
- Salt and pepper to taste

Instructions:

1. Put the Instant Pot in sauté mode and brown the ground beef.
2. Add the garlic and onion dice and cook until the onions are soft.
3. Add the oregano, cumin, and pepper powder and mix them in.
4. Tomato paste, black beans, kidney beans, and beef soup should all be added.
5. Add pepper and salt to taste.
6. Put the lid back on the Instant Pot and set it to high pressure for 10 minutes.
7. Let the pressure drop naturally for 10 minutes, then release any pressure by hand.
8. If you need to, change the seasonings and serve hot.

PAN-SEARED LEMON GARLIC TILAPIA:

Ingredients:

- 4 tilapia fillets
- 2 tablespoons olive oil
- 2 cloves garlic, minced
- Juice of 1 lemon
- Zest of 1 lemon
- 2 tablespoons fresh parsley, chopped
- Salt and pepper to taste

Instructions:

1. Use paper towels to dry the tilapia pieces, then season them with salt and pepper.
2. Warm up the olive oil in a big pan over medium-high heat.
3. Fry the garlic for one to two minutes until it smells good.
4. Flake the tilapia fillets with a fork after cooking them in the pan for three to four minutes on each side or until the fish is white.
5. Add lemon juice to the fillets just before they're done cooking.
6. Before you serve it, sprinkle lemon peel and fresh parsley on top.
7. Tilapia can be served with rice or any other side dish you like.

20-MINUTE BEEF AND BROCCOLI:

Ingredients:

- 1 lb (450g) flank steak, thinly sliced
- 1/2 cup soy sauce
- 1/4 cup oyster sauce
- 2 tablespoons brown sugar
- 2 tablespoons cornstarch
- 2 tablespoons vegetable oil
- 3 cups broccoli florets

- 3 cloves garlic, minced
- 1 teaspoon ginger, grated
- Sesame seeds and green onions for garnish (optional)
- Cooked rice for serving

Instructions:

1. Mix soy sauce, oyster sauce, brown sugar, and cornstarch in a spoonful bowl. Put away.
2. Put the vegetable oil in a big pan and heat it over medium-high heat.
3. Please put in the chopped flank steak and cook it until it turns brown. Take the steak out of the pan and set it aside.
4. If you need to, add more oil to the same pan. Cook the ginger and garlic until they smell good.
5. Put broccoli in the pan and stir-fry it for two to three minutes until it gets soft.
6. After cooking, put the steak back in the pan and pour the sauce over it. Make sure to mix everything well.
7. After that, cook for two to three minutes until the sauce gets thicker.
8. You can sprinkle sesame seeds and chopped green onions on top of the cooked rice before serving.

EASY CAPRESE CHICKEN SKILLET:

Ingredients:

- 4 boneless, skinless chicken breasts
- Salt and pepper to taste
- 1 tablespoon olive oil
- 1 cup cherry tomatoes, halved
- 1 cup fresh mozzarella balls, halved
- Balsamic glaze for drizzling

- Fresh basil leaves for garnish
- Cooked quinoa or pasta for serving

Instructions:

1. Add salt and pepper to the chicken breasts.
2. In a pan, heat the olive oil over medium-high heat. Please put in the chicken breasts and cook them until both sides are browned and fully cooked.
3. Take the chicken out of the pan and set it aside.
4. Put young tomatoes in the same pan and cook them until they soften.
5. Put the cooked chicken back in the pan. Put in the mozzarella balls and cook until the cheese starts to melt.
6. Put some balsamic glaze on top and add fresh basil leaves.
7. Put on top of cooked pasta or rice.

MEDITERRANEAN CHICKPEA WRAP RUSH:

Ingredients:

- 1 can (15 oz) chickpeas, drained and rinsed
- 1 cup cherry tomatoes, halved
- 1 cucumber, diced
- 1/2 red onion, finely chopped
- 1/4 cup Kalamata olives, sliced
- 1/4 cup feta cheese, crumbled
- 2 tablespoons olive oil
- 1 tablespoon red wine vinegar
- Salt and pepper to taste
- 4 whole-grain wraps

Instructions:

1. Put beans, cherry tomatoes, cucumber, red onion, olives, and feta cheese in a bowl.

2. Mix olive oil and red wine vinegar in a small bowl with a whisk. Add pepper and salt.
3. Add the sauce to the chickpea mix and mix it all by tossing.
4. Warm the wraps up in the oven or a dry pan.
5. Put some of the chickpea paste in the middle of each wrap.
6. Roll the wraps up by folding the sides over the centre.
7. Serve right away.

SPEEDY SAUSAGE AND PEPPERS:

Ingredients:

- 1 lb (450g) Italian sausage, sliced
- 1 tablespoon olive oil
- 1 onion, thinly sliced
- 2 bell peppers, thinly sliced (any colour)
- 2 cloves garlic, minced
- 1 teaspoon Italian seasoning
- Salt and pepper to taste
- Sub rolls for serving

Instructions:

1. Warm up the olive oil in a big pan over medium-high heat.
2. Put in the sausage slices and cook until all sides are brown.
3. Slice the peppers and onions and add them to the pan. Make sure the veggies are soft.
4. Add the Italian spice, salt, pepper, and minced garlic and mix them in. Add two more minutes of cooking.
5. Put the sausage and pepper mix on sub rolls to serve.

LEMON BUTTER SHRIMP PASTA:

Ingredients:

- 8 oz (225g) linguine or your favourite pasta
- 1 lb (450g) large shrimp, peeled and deveined
- 3 tablespoons unsalted butter
- 3 cloves garlic, minced
- 1/4 teaspoon red pepper flakes (optional)
- Zest of 1 lemon
- Juice of 1 lemon
- Salt and pepper to taste
- Fresh parsley, chopped (for garnish)

Instructions:

1. Follow the directions on the package to cook the pasta. Remove the water and set it aside.
2. Melt the butter in a big pan over medium-low heat. If you want, add red pepper flakes and chopped garlic. Sauté for one to two minutes until the garlic smells good.
3. Put the shrimp in the pan and cook them on each side for two to three minutes until they turn pink.
4. Add the lemon juice and zest, and mix well. Add pepper and salt to taste.
5. To ensure the pasta is properly covered with the lemon butter sauce, add it to the pan and toss it around.
6. Add fresh parsley on top and serve.

EXPRESS PESTO ZOODLES:

Ingredients:

- 4 medium zucchini, spiralized
- 1/2 cup store-bought pesto
- Cherry tomatoes, halved (for garnish)
- Grated Parmesan cheese (optional for serving)

Instructions:

1. To make zoodles, spiralize the zucchini.
2. Put the zoodles in a big skillet over medium-low heat. Cook for two to three minutes until they are just barely soft.
3. For the pesto sauce to fully coat the zoodles, add it and toss it around.
4. You can add cherry tomatoes and Parmesan cheese as a garnish if you want.
5. Serve right away.

QUICK AND HEALTHY TACO SALAD:

Ingredients:

- 1 lb (450g) ground turkey or lean ground beef
- 1 packet of taco seasoning
- 1 head of lettuce, shredded
- 1 cup cherry tomatoes, halved
- 1 cup black beans, drained and rinsed
- 1 cup corn kernels (fresh or frozen)
- 1 cup shredded cheddar cheese
- 1 avocado, diced
- Salsa and Greek yoghurt (optional for serving)

Instructions:

1. Put the ground turkey or beef in a pan and cook it over medium-low heat until it turns brown. Get rid of extra fat.
2. Following the directions on the package, add taco sauce.
3. Put a big bowl of black beans, corn, shredded cheese, cherry tomatoes, and shredded lettuce.
4. Put the chunks of cooked meat, salsa, Greek yoghurt, and avocado on the salad.

5. Mix everything, then serve.

FAST AND FLAVORFUL FRIED RICE:

Ingredients:

- 3 cups cooked rice (preferably chilled)
- 2 tablespoons vegetable oil
- 1 cup cooked and diced chicken (or shrimp, tofu, or your choice of protein)
- 1 cup mixed vegetables (peas, carrots, corn)
- 2 eggs, beaten
- 3 tablespoons soy sauce
- 1 teaspoon sesame oil
- Green onions, chopped (for garnish)

Instructions:

1. Heat vegetable oil in a big pan or wok over medium-high heat.
2. Please put in the chicken pieces and cook until they turn brown.
3. As you pour the eggs into the pan, move the chicken to the side. Make sure the eggs are fully cooked.
4. Put the mixed vegetables in the pan and stir-fry them for two to three minutes.
5. Soy sauce, olive oil, and cold rice should all be added. Mix everything until it's all well mixed and hot.
6. Add some chopped green onions on top and serve.

15-MINUTE GARLIC BUTTER CHICKEN:

Ingredients:

- 4 boneless, skinless chicken breasts
- 4 tablespoons unsalted butter

- 4 cloves garlic, minced
- 1 teaspoon dried thyme
- 1 teaspoon dried rosemary
- Salt and pepper to taste
- Fresh parsley for garnish

Instructions:

1. On both sides, salt and pepper the chicken breasts.
2. While the pan is on medium-high heat, melt 2 tablespoons of butter.
3. Put the chicken breasts in the pan and cook them on each side for 5 to 6 minutes or until the temperature inside hits 165°F (74°C).
4. To finish cooking, add the chopped garlic, thyme, and rosemary to the pan in the last two minutes. The garlic and herbs should be mixed into the chicken.
5. Take the chicken out of the pan and set it away when fully cooked.
6. Melt the last 2 tablespoons of butter in the pan, scraping up any brown bits on the bottom.
7. Put the garlic butter on the cooked chicken, add fresh parsley, and serve.

RAPID RATATOUILLE STIR-FRY:

Ingredients:

- 1 eggplant, diced
- 1 zucchini, diced
- 1 yellow bell pepper, diced
- 1 red onion, thinly sliced
- 2 tomatoes, diced
- 3 tablespoons olive oil
- 3 cloves garlic, minced

- 1 teaspoon dried oregano
- Salt and pepper to taste
- Fresh basil for garnish

Instructions:

1. Heat the olive oil over medium-high heat

in a big pan or wok.

2. Please put in the garlic and cook for one minute until it smells good.
3. Cut up the onion, bell pepper, zucchini, and eggplant and add them to the pan. For five to seven minutes, or until the veggies are soft but still crisp, stir-fry them.
4. Mix in the dried oregano, salt, pepper, and tomato slices. Mix everything, then cook for another two to three minutes.
5. Check the spices and make changes if needed.
6. Before serving, sprinkle with fresh basil.

DESSERTS WITH A TWIST:

MATCHA GREEN TEA TIRAMISU:

Ingredients:

- 1 cup strong brewed matcha green tea, cooled
- 3 tablespoons matcha powder
- 4 large egg yolks
- 1 cup granulated sugar
- 1 1/2 cups mascarpone cheese
- 1 cup heavy cream
- 1 teaspoon vanilla extract
- 24-30 ladyfinger cookies

- Cocoa powder for dusting

Instructions:

1. Mix the hot matcha tea and matcha powder in a bowl. Put away.
2. Mix the egg whites and sugar in a different bowl with a whisk until the mixture is thick and pale.
3. Add the mascarpone cheese to the egg yolk mix and mix it in until it's smooth.
4. Mix the heavy cream and vanilla extract in a different bowl and beat them together until hard peaks form.
5. Mix the mascarpone and whipped cream by folding them in slowly.
6. Each ladyfinger should be dipped in the matcha tea mixture and then stacked at the base of a serving dish.
7. Add half of the mascarpone mixture to the ladyfingers and spread it out.
8. Use the rest of the ladyfingers and mascarpone mixture to make more layers.
9. Please put it in the fridge for at least four hours or overnight with the lid on.
10. To serve, sprinkle the chocolate powder over the top.

LAVENDER HONEY PEACH COBBLER:

Ingredients:

- 6 cups fresh peaches, peeled and sliced
- 1/4 cup honey
- 2 tablespoons fresh lavender flowers (or 1 tablespoon dried)
- 1 cup all-purpose flour
- 1 cup granulated sugar
- 1 teaspoon baking powder

- 1/2 teaspoon salt
- 1 cup milk
- 1/2 cup unsalted butter, melted
- Vanilla ice cream for serving (optional)

Instructions:

1. Warm the oven up to 190°C (375°F).
2. Put sliced peaches, honey, and lavender in a big bowl. Let it sit for 15 minutes after you toss it to coat it.
3. Mix the flour, sugar, baking powder, and salt in a different bowl using a whisk.
4. Add the milk and melting butter and mix them in well.
5. Put the batter into a baking dish that has been greased.
6. Put the fruit mix on top of the batter.
7. Bake for 40 to 45 minutes until the peaches bubble and the top turns golden brown.
8. Let it cool down a bit before you serve it. If you want, you can serve it with vanilla ice cream.

CHOCOLATE AVOCADO TRUFFLES:

Ingredients:

- 2 ripe avocados
- 1/2 cup cocoa powder
- 1/4 cup maple syrup or honey
- 1 teaspoon vanilla extract
- A pinch of salt
- Shredded coconut, chopped nuts, or cocoa powder for coating

Instructions:

1. Put the cocoa powder, honey, maple syrup, vanilla extract, and a pinch of salt in a food processor and blend them.
2. Mix until it's creamy and smooth.
3. Put the mixture in the fridge for at least 30 minutes to cool it down.
4. Take small amounts and make them into truffles.
5. Roll them in chocolate powder, shredded coconut, or chopped nuts

to cover the truffles.

6. Please put it back in the fridge for another 30 minutes before serving.

CARDAMOM ROSEWATER RICE PUDDING:

Ingredients:

- 1 cup Arborio rice
- 4 cups whole milk
- 1/2 cup sugar
- 1 teaspoon ground cardamom
- 1 teaspoon rosewater
- 1/4 cup chopped pistachios for garnish

Instructions:

1. Put the rice, milk, and sugar in a medium pot.
2. Stir often as you bring it to a simmer over medium heat.
3. Turn down the heat and simmer for 25 to 30 minutes, or until the rice is soft and the sauce thickens.
4. Add rosewater and ground cardamom and mix well.
5. Take it off the heat and let it cool down a bit.
6. Add chopped pistachios on top and serve warm.

HIBISCUS BERRY SORBET SWIRL:

Ingredients:

- 2 cups hibiscus tea, brewed and cooled
- 1 cup mixed berries (strawberries, blueberries, raspberries)
- 1/2 cup sugar
- 1 tablespoon lemon juice

Instructions:

1. Put the hibiscus tea, mixed berries, sugar, and lemon juice in a blender.
2. Mix until it's smooth.
3. Put the mix in a small pan and freeze it for two hours.
4. After two hours, break up any ice crystals with a fork and stir the mixture around.
5. Freeze for another 4 to 6 hours or until it sets.
6. Enjoy it in bowls or cones.

EARL GREY INFUSED CHOCOLATE MOUSSE:

Ingredients:

- 1 cup heavy cream
- 4 Earl Grey tea bags
- 8 ounces dark chocolate, chopped
- 3 tablespoons sugar
- 4 large eggs, separated
- 1 teaspoon vanilla extract

Instructions:

1. Just before it boils, heat the heavy cream. Add the Earl Grey tea bags and let them soak in the hot cream for 10

minutes. Take the tea bags out of the cream and let it cool down.

2. You can melt the dark chocolate in the oven or over simmering water in a bowl that can handle heat.
3. Mix the sugar and egg yolks in a different bowl until the yolks are pale and smooth.
4. Slowly add the melted chocolate to the egg yolk mixture and mix it well after each addition.
5. Mix the vanilla extract into the chocolate.
6. Whip the cream with Earl Grey in it until stiff peaks form.
7. Add the whipped cream to the chocolate mixture slowly.
8. Mix the egg whites in a different bowl and beat them until they form hard peaks. Then, fold the egg whites into the chocolate mixture.
9. Put the mousse in glasses to serve and put them in the fridge for at least 4 hours or until the mousse sets.

PISTACHIO ROSE SEMOLINA CAKE:

Ingredients:

- 1 cup semolina
- 1 cup pistachios, finely ground
- 1 cup sugar
- 1 cup plain yogurt
- 1/2 cup vegetable oil
- 1/4 cup rose water
- 1 teaspoon baking powder
- 1/2 teaspoon baking soda
- A pinch of salt

Instructions:

1. Warm the oven up to 175°F (350°F). Butter and flour in a cake pan.

2. Put sugar, baking powder, baking soda, ground almonds, semolina, and salt in a bowl.
3. Mix yoghurt, vegetable oil, and rose water in a different bowl.
4. Slowly add the wet ingredients to the dry ones until everything is well-mixed.
5. Pour the batter into the ready cake pan and smooth the top

6. Please put it in the oven and bake for 30 to 35 minutes or until a toothpick stuck in the middle comes out clean.
7. Let the cake cool down before cutting it up and serving it.

LEMON BASIL SHORTBREAD COOKIES:

Ingredients:

- 1 cup unsalted butter, softened
- 1/2 cup powdered sugar
- 2 cups all-purpose flour
- Zest of 2 lemons
- 2 tablespoons fresh basil, finely chopped
- A pinch of salt

Instructions:

1. Warm the oven up to 160°C/325°F. Put parchment paper on the bottom of a baking sheet.
2. Mix the butter and powdered sugar in a big bowl until the mixture is light and fluffy.
3. Put in the basil leaves, lemon juice, flour, and a little salt. Mix the dough until it holds together.
4. Make a ball out of the dough and cover it with plastic wrap. Please put it in the fridge for at least an hour.

5. Cut the cold dough into thin slices before putting the cookies on the baking sheet.
6. For 12 to 15 minutes, or until the edges begin to brown.
7. Let the cookies cool for a few minutes on the baking sheet before moving them to a wire rack to cool all the way.

BALSAMIC STRAWBERRY BASIL TART:

Ingredients:

For the crust:

- 1 1/2 cups all-purpose flour
- 1/2 cup unsalted butter, cold and cubed
- 1/4 cup granulated sugar
- 1/4 teaspoon salt
- 2-3 tablespoons cold water

For the filling:

- 2 cups fresh strawberries, hulled and sliced
- 1/4 cup balsamic vinegar
- 1/4 cup granulated sugar
- 1 tablespoon fresh basil, chopped

Instructions:

1. Warm the oven up to 190°C (375°F).
2. Blend the flour, butter, sugar, and salt in a food processor for the crust. Pulse the ingredients together until they look like big crumbs.
3. One tablespoon of cold water should be added and pulsed into the dough until it comes together.
4. Fill a pie pan with dough and press it to cover the bottom and sides. A fork should be used to poke holes in the

bottom. Bake for 15 to 20 minutes or until golden brown. Let it cool down.

5. To make the filling, put strawberries, balsamic vinegar, sugar, and basil in a bowl and mix them. Wait 15 minutes.
6. Put the fruit mix into the tart crust and leave to cool.
7. Please put it in the fridge for at least an hour before you serve it.

ORANGE CARDAMOM PANNA COTTA:

Ingredients:

- 2 cups heavy cream
- 1/2 cup whole milk
- 1/2 cup granulated sugar
- Zest of 1 orange
- 1 teaspoon ground cardamom
- 2 teaspoons vanilla extract
- 2 1/2 teaspoons gelatin
- 3 tablespoons cold water

Instructions:

1. Mix heavy cream, milk, sugar, orange juice, and cardamom in a saucepan. Start cooking it on medium heat and wait for it to boil. Then, take it off the heat.
2. It takes 5 minutes for the gelatin to dissolve in the cold water in a small bowl.
3. Add the gelatin mixture to the warm cream mixture and mix it in until it's all melted.
4. Pour in the vanilla syrup.
5. Separate the orange juice from the mixture using a filter.
6. Put the mix into glasses or shapes that can hold individual servings.
7. Place in the fridge for at least four hours or until it sets.

SPICED PEAR AND WALNUT GALETTE:

Ingredients:

For the crust:

- 1 1/4 cups all-purpose flour
- 1/2 cup unsalted butter, cold and cubed
- 1 tablespoon granulated sugar
- 1/4 teaspoon salt
- 3-4 tablespoons cold water

For the filling:

- 3 ripe pears, thinly sliced
- 1/4 cup granulated sugar
- 1 teaspoon ground cinnamon
- 1/2 cup chopped walnuts

Instructions:

1. Warm the oven up to 190°C (375°F).
2. Add the flour, butter, sugar, and salt to a food processor and pulse it a few times to make coarse crumbs for the top.
3. One tablespoon of cold water should be added and pulsed until the dough forms.
4. On a greased surface, roll the dough into a circle.
5. Put sliced pears, sugar, cinnamon, and walnuts in a bowl.
6. In the middle of the rolled-out dough, put the pear mixture. Leave some space around the sides.
7. Fold the dough's ends over the pear filling

to make a rustic galette.

8. Please put it in the oven for 30 to 35 minutes or until the top turns golden brown.
9. Let it cool down a bit before you serve it.

BLUEBERRY BASIL FROZEN YOGURT:

Ingredients:

- 2 cups fresh or frozen blueberries
- 1/2 cup granulated sugar
- 2 cups plain Greek yogurt
- 1/4 cup honey
- 2 tablespoons fresh basil, finely chopped
- 1 tablespoon lemon juice

Instructions:

1. Blueberries and sugar should be put in a blender. Mix until it's smooth.
2. Put the blueberry mix, Greek yoghurt, honey, basil, and lemon juice in a bowl.
3. Put the liquid into an ice cream maker and churn it as directed by the maker's maker.
4. After churning, put the frozen yoghurt in a jar with a lid and freeze it for two more hours to make it firm.
5. Place the frozen yoghurt on a plate and top it with fresh blueberries and basil.

CINNAMON CHILI CHOCOLATE FONDUE:

Ingredients:

- 8 ounces (about 225g) dark chocolate, chopped
- 1 cup heavy cream
- 1 teaspoon ground cinnamon
- 1/2 teaspoon chilli powder

- Assorted dippables (strawberries, banana slices, marshmallows, pretzels, etc.)

Instructions:

1. Put the heavy cream and chopped chocolate in a pot and heat it over low heat.
2. Keep stirring the mixture until the chocolate melts, and it's smooth.
3. Mix the ground cinnamon and pepper powder with a spoon.
4. Move the chocolate mix to a bowl for serving or a fondue pot.
5. Serve with a variety of dippables.

GINGER TURMERIC MANGO SORBET:

Ingredients:

- 4 cups frozen mango chunks
- 1/2 cup fresh orange juice
- 1 tablespoon fresh ginger, grated
- 1 teaspoon ground turmeric
- 1/2 cup honey or maple syrup

Instructions:

1. Put frozen mango chunks, fresh orange juice, chopped ginger, ground turmeric, honey or maple syrup, and blend them in a blender.
2. Mix until it's creamy and smooth.
3. It should be frozen for at least 4 hours or overnight after you pour it into a small dish.
4. Let the sorbet sit at room temperature for a few minutes to get softer before serving it.
5. Serve with a scoop.

RASPBERRY MINT CHOCOLATE BARK:

Ingredients:

- 8 ounces (about 225g) dark chocolate, melted
- 1/2 cup fresh raspberries
- 2 tablespoons fresh mint, chopped

Instructions:

1. Put parchment paper on the bottom of a baking sheet.
2. Spread the melted dark chocolate out evenly on the parchment paper.
3. Place fresh raspberries on top of the chocolate and top with chopped mint.
4. After about an hour, put the baking sheet in the fridge so the chocolate sets.
5. Break the chocolate into pieces and serve after it has set.

ESPRESSO HAZELNUT AFFOGATO:

Ingredients:

- 2 shots of espresso
- 4 scoops vanilla ice cream
- 2 tablespoons chopped hazelnuts (toasted, if desired)

Instructions:

1. Make two coffee shots.
2. Each bowl or glass should have a scoop of vanilla ice cream.
3. For each scoop of ice cream, add a shot of espresso.
4. Add chopped walnuts on top.
5. Serve immediately and enjoy how good hot espresso and ice cream taste together.

www.ingramcontent.com/pod-product-compliance
Lightning Source LLC
LaVergne TN
LVHW050827230925
821698LV00056B/350